I0437243

DR. PIERRE F. WALTER

PROCESSED REALITY

Pitfalls of Perception and the Cosmic Mind

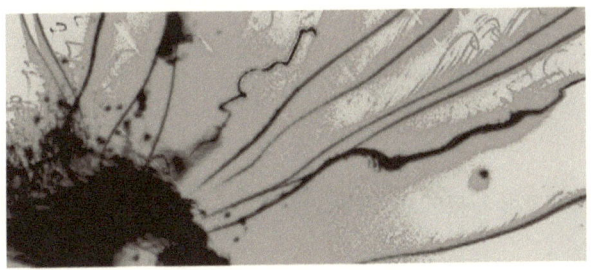

"Essays Series"

Published by Sirius-C Media Galaxy LLC

http://sirius-c-publishing.com

http://authoryourlife.com

http://siriuscmedia.com

http://blissviews.com

http://ipublica.com

http://ipublica.net

ISBN 978-1-475256-49-9

Contact Information Dr. Pierre F. Walter

publisher@sirius-c-publishing.com

About Dr. Pierre F. Walter

http://drpfw.info

Quotation Suggestion

Pierre F. Walter, *Processed Reality: Pitfalls of Perception and the Cosmic Mind,* Newark: Sirius-C Media Galaxy LLC, 2012

About the Author

Dr. Pierre F. Walter is an author, international lawyer, researcher, corporate trainer, and lecturer. After finalizing studies in German Law, International Law and *European integration* with diplomas obtained in 1981 through 1983, he graduated in December 1987 at the Law Faculty of the University of Geneva as *Docteur en Droit* in international law.

The doctorate was funded by scholarships from the *Swiss Institute of Comparative Law*, Lausanne, and from the *University of Geneva*, as well as a Fulbright Travel Grant for an assistantship with Professor Louis B. Sohn at *UGA Law School Department of International Law,* Athens, Georgia, USA, in 1985. Pierre F. Walter also served as a research assistant to *Freshfields, Bruckhaus, Deringer,* Cologne, Germany in 1983 and to *Lalive Lawyers,* Geneva, in 1987.

Pierre F. Walter writes and lectures in English, German and French languages; he has written *more than ten thousand pages* embracing all literary genres, including *novels, short stories, film scripts, essays, selfhelp books, monographs* and extended *book reviews*. Also a pianist and composer, he has realized 40 CDs with *jazz, newage* and *relaxation music*.

Pierre F. Walter's professional publications span the domains *International Law, Criminal Law, Holistic Science, Psychology, Education, Shamanism, Ecology, Spirituality, Quantum Physics, Systems Theory, Natural Healing, Peace Research, Personal Growth, Selfhelp* and *Consciousness Research*. 110 Book Reviews, forty audio books and more than one hundred fifty video lectures were realized in the years 2005-2010. Besides, Pierre F. Walter is author and editor of *Great Minds Series (2010), Scholarly Articles Series (2011)* and *Essays Series (2012)*.

Pierre F. Walter publishes via his Delaware firm *Sirius-C Media Galaxy LLC* and the imprints IPUBLICA and Sirius-C Media (SCM).

To Nelson

CONTENTS

All of you will need to heal, decode, rescript and reprogram, so that fear is no longer a part of your psyche.
– Wendy Munro, *Journey into a New Millennium (1997)*

INTRODUCTION

One of the essential questions I am asking in this essay is what conditioning is, why humans have a strong tendency to be conditioned to all kinds of social rules and norms, how conditioning is effected and what purpose it serves.

As a second step, then I try to make out some hidden connections between conditioning, perception and cognition.

To begin with, I am asking upfront if it is at all possible to enjoy reality *unprocessed*, as raw information that comes in through the senses, or if reality as we perceive it *is already a processed one* in the sense that it is distorted by our perception interface, and therefore, conditioned? Hence, when we want to find out about the subtle techniques of cultural conditioning, we better look first into its contrary and ask: what is that state that is *not* conditioned. This leads us automatically to the question what *reality* is. Is reality a matter of perception? Or rather a matter of beliefs? How do our beliefs impact and imprint upon our perception? What makes us believe at all?

Do we need to believe anything? Or is making up beliefs perhaps an automatism of our brain?

Is reality rational, irrational or meta–rational? Do we live in different realities or is there one single monolithic reality?

Further, can we perceive reality in a pure, unprocessed state or is every reality we perceive a 'processed reality' already, namely in the sense that our perception is conditioned by the feedback–loop of our memory surface? And can we clear our perception surface to a point to perceive reality, whatever it takes to get there, in a pure and unprocessed state? Is the universe a creation of our thoughts, or is it an abstract creation? What about *poetic* reality? How is it possible that great poets and thinkers have intuited most of the findings that quantum physics now reveals to us?

And once we have clarity about how perception works, and how easily it is manipulated by the big commercial and political players, we may inquire into that latest slogan they have come up with some years ago, and that reads *worldwide democracy*. And we may ask: 'What is that soup and what is the taste of it?'

What is *worldwide democracy* and in which ways does it infringe upon our perception of reality? And upon which *myths* is it built?

These are some of the questions I try to ask and answer as good as I can in this essay. By the way, those who see the solution of all problems in the propagation of what they call *rational reality* or *logical reality* are mistaken as they blind out the irrational, which is equally part of human nature. Our emotions have their own intelligence, and yet they are *not* rational when perceived only from the left side of the river, our deductive mind. We have a right brain hemisphere, and that functions pretty much on the irrational side most of the time, and through associative logic.[1]

We cannot perceive the *totality of reality* as long as we blind out a part of our human setup. *We are totally aware when we are totally human*. And we are totally inhuman when we are

---

[1] http://ipublica.net/brain-research/

totally rational. The intelligence of nature is not rational, but meta–rational or holistic.

Let us have an overview over 1960s and 70s neurological research and the early theory of 'preferred pathways', proposed by neurologist Herbert James Campbell in his book *The Pleasure Areas (1973)*, as well as the 'mechanism of mind' theory of think tank Edward de Bono.[2] We see that this research clearly suggests that the brain 'can only see what it already knows' (Edward de Bono) and that as a result, researchers can only pick out the data from their research that confirms their basic assumptions and beliefs.

This research thus anticipated the basic tenet of quantum physics that however we set up an experiment, the observer shall always be entangled with the object he observes. In addition, this mechanism of our brain, which serves survival, not the highest possible accuracy of perception, makes for fundamental novelty most of the time brought about by accidents, mistakes, lapses of attention, and the like, because as long as the mechanism of our brain is intact, we cannot experience novelty.

Does that mean that the door is closed forever in the sense that direct perception is an impossibility? Despite this setup of our perception interface, direct perception is possible, while it's possible only for a select few of shamans, yogis, zen masters and generally, people who have really worked through their emotional entanglements, and who reduced

---

[2] http://ipublica.net/herbert-james-campbell/
http://ipublica.net/edward-de-bono/

their projections and blown–up belief system to a strict minimum. As we thus can acknowledge that direct perception is possible, we can ask what the precise criteria are for it to happen? We see, based on this insight, that we are actually educated in our culture to misuse our brains and to develop a faulty perception interface.

In an attempt to define Love, Krishnamurti once said that Love cannot be defined, or it becomes a concept; thus to understand Love, we can only approach it negatively, looking at all what is *not* Love.[3] This is the approach I am taking in this essay, showing with a number of present–day examples, that what is generally taken for 'reality' is a 'processed food' in the sense that it's pervaded with concepts, ideological, religious or scientific, and thus data that is not part of the original idea.

To remind one of the several examples of 'myths' I am going to present further down in this essay, *child protection*, we can see that originally, the idea was to protect children from harm, as simple and as effective as this sounds.[4] But then, when we look at what 'child protection' really does, what it really leads to in our society, what it really implies, what it really results in, then we see that it creates more harm to children than the situation when children go unprotected, that it creates *more confusion and more violence* than any given society would experience that doesn't care, or cares to a lesser

---

[3] http://ipublica.net/j-krishnamurti/
http://ipublica.net/love/

[4] http://ipublica.net/child-protection/

extent, at protecting their children in an organized and poli-ce–backed manner. And last not least, we see that this para-digm really interferes with children's natural sexual growth in that it demonizes and persecutes any attempt of a child to experience sexual pleasure with another child or an adult, thus pervading the early environment of children with fear, a real fear of life that can develop into hysteria and paranoia, and can in extreme cases lead to autism, learning disabilities, anorexia, depressions, epilepsy, and even schizophrenia.

Taking a kind of bird perspective, we can only wonder how a society can declare itself to being 'scientific' and 'en-lightened', compared to a *religiously fundamentalist* regime, and nonetheless bring about a reality that is composed of exactly the same elements that fundamentalist regimes are putting in place, such as strong fear of authority, meticulous state su-pervision ruling into human relations, and especially, the family, large–scale prohibitions targeting primarily at human intimacy, speech taboos, large–scale censorship of 'sensitive' issues such as adult–child sexual behavior, and draconian punishments waiting for the law breaker. And we can only wonder how such a society can be so bold and daring to sell this mix of violence, state–ordained brutality, ignorance, ma-nipulation and suppression of non–system–conform re-search, taboo–thinking, retrograde provincialism and fascism in a garment called 'worldwide democracy'?

To remind my base intention when writing this essay, it was not meant as a pamphlet or social critique, or else a form of political activism. If this had been the cause, it would have been published in a different manner; hence my base intention was to present the data as a consciousness opener.

If such doing is possible in just any kind of society, be it based upon religious or agnostic fundamentalism, then something must be basically wrong with how we handle perception, with how we see and evaluate reality, with how we are brought up, with how we have learnt to handle reality. Then we need to actually reframe our perceptions and clear our perception interface; we might also want to take a role in the educational or political world so as to work against ignorance and for fostering *real information*, one namely that is based on correct perception, perception that is as direct and pure as possible, perception that is as much as possible *free of contamination*, of lies, of political maneuvering, and opportunism.

Hence it is of paramount importance how we handle our perception interface; from this insight, we can then set about to improve self–reflective consciousness, to build awareness of our thinking habits and behavior patterns, and see how our actions impact *upon society as a whole*, considering karma for a whole group, or even a nation, or the entire globe. When we do this, we see that we are *responsible*, through the very fact of participating in creation and co–creation, or as Dr. William Tiller[5] put it in the movie 'What the Bleep Do We Know!?, in our being 'avatars'.[6] This, then, will shift our regard and deprive us from comforting projections such as 'our government is the culprit' or 'modern–time debauchery and lack of

---

[5] http://ipublica.net/william-tiller/

[6] http://ipublica.net/what-the-bleep-do-we-know/

values is the culprit' or 'lack of religious belonging is the culprit'. We then see that the universe doesn't ask who is a culprit for anything that ever happened, but asks us to stay true to the basic principle in a responsive universe, that is, *individual response–ability*.

This, in turn, leads to a careful approach when meeting ourselves, in our daily self–talk, when meeting others in our daily dialogues and exchanges, and in our cooperation with others. The starting point always is *how we perceive reality*, and how we *still better* perceive reality when being meticulous, just like a warrior, in keeping our perception interface as pure and pristine as possible.

PROCESSING REALITY

This chapter on *consciousness research* questions the onto-logical validity of cultural, social or moral conditioning and throws us back to apprehending our true *soul values*, both on an individual and a group level. Our first topic of inquiry is the question if the human mind is able to perceive the *crude unprocessed reality* as is – or if it inevitably needs to process it?

In other words, can we eat the soup of life without putting salt in it, and without heating it up? Is it possible to perceive reality other than through the opaque filter of our conditioned mind? Can the mind be cleansed for better perception, or else altogether *circumvented* during the process of perception? Can perception be pure and undistorted in the sense of being *direct and immediate?*

Before I try to give answers to these questions further down in *Creating Reality*, let us first see the mechanism of our mind when perceiving reality; this implies the process of *perception* and also the question how the brain, as the long arm of our mind, handles the information which is received.

It is today agreed upon among the majority of neurologists and consciousness explorers that the mind and the brain are both necessary in the *process of perception*. The mind is the larger framework and perceives the whole of reality, while the brain seems to be a functional unit of the mind, more involved with the actual information processing.

Much is still open here, but one thing is sure: the mind and the brain are not, what was thought still some decades ago, one and the same thing. The mind can be imagined as the *matrix*, and the brain as the *processing device*. But we must not functionally confuse them as their roles in perception are clearly set by nature, and this was formerly a *terra incognita* in science and came to be known only by modern neurology in combination with the insights we gained from mind–opening and consciousness transforming psychedelic experiences.

The process of learning, if we want to understand it intelligently, can only be grasped when we look at the *totality* of perception. Learning is the way we deal with what we perceive, it is a process of *processing information* and this information is collected by our brain through a rather complicated process that we call *perception*. Thus, when we care about the process of learning, the way we learn, we need to look at what perception is and how it works.

Perception is a topic not very broadly discussed in modern science. This obvious neglect of scientific in–depth study into the holistic process of perception has various reasons.

The main reason is the general focus of modern science upon *information processing*. There was a *historic shift* around the end of Antiquity that led to a trend away from direct perception and toward information processing, archiving or mere information reproduction, that I call *Historical Turn Toward Stupidity*.

That is why today we have collectively forgotten about direct perception. Yet this knowledge has survived in *shamanism* and with spiritual healers in South America, Asia and Africa, and generally with native peoples. And it is part of a perennial spiritual tradition among sages in the East and the West.

What, then, is *direct perception?*

Direct perception is our natural and most intelligent mode of perception. It is perception that circumvents most of the information processing circuits and therefore leaves the incoming signal as untouched and intact as possible.[7]

New research has fully corroborated the teachings of the old sages who said that learning has to be holistic and whole-brain in order to be truly effective. To look deeper into these facts, we cannot get around the disturbing insight that since about the scientific doctrine of *Aristotle*, and within Occidental culture, we have used our brains in the wrong way.[8]

You may laugh but I am serious when I say that there is another abuse you haven't heard about yet: it's *brain abuse*. And it's a cultural thing. We as a culture have misused our brains, billions of brains in billions of people.

We do that by educating children in the wrong way, in a way to systematically abuse of their brains, until they do it the way we other adults do it, by using only about four to eight per cent of their brain potential. Now, we hardly got time to sit around crying. I would say that there was never a better time for us, as individuals, as a group, as a nation, as humanity, to really see this fact as it is and to work on the *reformation of culture.* To turn it upside down. So that the garbage falls out, and all the wrong beliefs. How to turn culture

---

[7] http://ipublica.net/direct-perception/

[8] http://ipublica.net/aristotle/

upside down? By studying it, deeply, thoroughly, with all our energy. This culture is in us, in our cells, in our brains, in our skin, in our stomachs. We cannot just vomit it out for being newborn as a *tabula rasa*.

Metaphorically speaking, it's not by throwing bombs in McDonald restaurants that you get free from the murder culture. It's by accepting *all* the ingredients of this culture. Thus, by going to a good restaurant, eating with good table manners, and selecting fresh food, by using the napkin and patiently, and lovingly, teaching your children to do the same, you reform and transform culture.

It's because you renew it by *really absorbing it*. What you do, instead, is to pay lip–service to it and then go to eat like a pig. And then, after a while of indulging in pighood, you wonder why your children become pigs.

You think that when you let your children grow into a no–culture, you give them freedom and options, right? Not so. *You give them violence, chaos and a no–option mindset.* Your children can only grow in culture. And that culture is *your* culture. Tell me in which culture they should grow if not in yours?

So, when I follow your logic, we both can only agree about this: your children will grow in no culture. You do not teach them your own culture because you think it's a messy kind of thing, too violent, not really conscious, manipulative. *Yes, it is all that.* But, you cannot turn the culture upside–down by rejecting it. You can only turn it around by ingesting it – and then, once you have also digested it, by *overcoming* it.

When you know what culture is all about, you can choose *another culture* to live in.

We can only wonder when we hear scientists say that generally we use only five to eight percent of our brain or creative resources. Why are we so terribly unproductive, so utterly ineffective in our creativity, in our performance, in our achievements? Despite this whole process called *civilization*, despite schools, colleges and universities, despite the printing press, Gutenberg and all the rest of it, we have remained in a truly *primitive state of evolution* regarding learning and understanding the learning process.

The answer is dead simple. It's because we live without culture. And this, in turn, is so because quite without reflecting about it, we have never really accepted that culture into which we were born and that is *ours*. I am not really concerned with finding out about the causes or reasons for this tremendous waste of opportunity, but well with the possibilities to change this state of affairs on an individual human level.

The world changes through multiple and repeated changes on an individual level. Once a sufficient number of individuals have done their quantum leap to a higher evolutionary vibration, there will be a major paradigm shift in the whole system that makes that group or collective consciousness, too, will reproduce this shift on the group, national or global level. This is how all true civilization comes about: all begins in the cell and then expands to bigger patterns. Nature is coded in *patterns* that are holistically related to each other and where the information of the whole is contained in every single cell of the pattern.[9]

The pattern structure is the model for the information the brain receives and stores. New information is added–on to existing information. Without this kind of information routing, which is part of the brain's mechanism of information processing, that in neurology is called *preferred pathways*, memory would not be possible.

The better the brain can manage to associate new input with existing patterns of information, the faster the information storage will be, and thus the higher will be the memorization result.

Our brain does this intake of information automatically, passively, without a need for us to set a decision about it. This fact is tremendously important for the understanding of the functioning of the brain. There is namely a *positive side* and a *negative side* about it. Positively, the passively organizing perception structure of the brain insures that we continuously receive and store information; we cannot 'shut down' the brain. Even in coma or deep hypnosis we perceive and register all that goes on around us. All the information from the five, and I would correct, the six senses is perceived and stored in the subconscious memory surface that never sleeps, and that perhaps, at least in a condensed fashion, also survives death. So the apparently passive functioning of the brain is actually a vividly active process. The important point

---

[9] See Pierre F. Walter, *Eight Dynamic Patterns of Living: Base Elements of True Civilization*, Scholarly Article (2011).

about it is that the organizer of the information is inside and not outside of the system. To give an example, let us have a look at two groups of children. The *first group* is raised permissively so that they can pick up any information freely from their environment and grow, from the information they get, into what they are individually destined for.

The *second group*, however, is strictly regulated, protected and warded off from any unprocessed information. Which group, would you think, will be more intelligent and more creative, the first or the second one? Of course the first one. Simply because in their case the freely organizing system of their perception and the free flow of information, combined with high input will make their brains working on high gear from early age, whereas in the second group creative learning processes are for the most part impaired, blocked or even mutilated.

In the first group the organizer of the information is *inside*, within the children, while in the second group it is *outside*, and in the tutelary adults around the children, their parents and teachers for the most part, that are putting up valves for the free flow of incoming information, filtering out the larger part of it. We can also put it that way: in the first group it is *nature's intelligence* that cares for the children's evolution, in the second case it is limited and rather shortsighted human willfulness. This simple example shows the high impact the early environment has on the development of our intelligence and our later use of the potential that we've got.

In my opinion we all have got high or exceptional potential but only very few of us were exposed to the right environmental support and have, in addition, developed the necessary creative will to free themselves from the dangers of conditioning. And we need both those factors working in a positive sense if we are to fully develop our talents and creative powers.

J. Krishnamurti, today recognized as one of humanity's most important spiritual teachers, was as a child constantly beaten in school by a stupid and ignorant teacher. His childhood was all misery and solitude and he would probably have ended as the village idiot if the Theosophists had not discovered the boy and taken him to England where he was educated under their patronage. [10]

Announced by seers as the *New Messiahs*, this boy was found, at age fourteen, at a beach in Bangalore, South India, neglected, almost toothless, malnourished and sad. Krishnamurti, as a little boy, rejected the knowledge he was supposed to assimilate. He rejected all of it, the whole of conditioning, societal, religious, moral or whatever.

And because of this refusal he was treated with utter disrespect and violence, as so many children who, like him, prefer to remain *in their original state of mind* which is pure and unspoiled, the mind of a totally conscious direct observer.

Krishnamurti learned by direct perception and therefore his learning was immediate, perfectly spontaneous and almost instantaneous: the whole–brain learning of a genius.

Direct perception is the key to using our hidden potential in hitherto unforeseen ways that allow us to bring about un-

---

[10] http://ipublica.net/theosophy/

usual capacities that we know only from people who are either called yogis or geniuses. However, we are all gifted with the spark of the Divine and able to pass beyond the limitations of our conditioned mind.

PITFALLS OF PERCEPTION

Edward de Bono was one of the first coaches and professional think tanks who, after thorough research into the functioning of the brain and human perception, found that *human perception is faulty in the sense that its self–organizing structure is conditioned to ensure survival*, and not to bring about the highest possible level of integrity in processing and storing the data that is coming in through the senses.

When the brain receives new information, it has only *two alternatives* for storing that information away; it builds a new pattern or adds the data on to an existing pattern. The first alternative would ensure the highest level of preserving the integrity of the incoming information. The second alternative ultimately brings about a faulty perception interface, but it's much faster to process for the brain, and it serves survival because it builds upon already established information pathways in the brain.

The Memory Matrix

When de Bono, in 1969, released his theory of passively organizing systems in one of his first books, *The Mechanism of Mind (1969),* scientists at first disregarded his research. [11]

When later Nobel prize winners confirmed it, and amazing new discoveries in neurology corroborated it, de Bono became well–known and his advice was sought after by some of the largest corporations in the world.

---

[11] Edward de Bono, *The Mechanism of Mind (1969).*

The preferred–pathways theory, now presented even in popular science books, is the scientific formulation of de Bono's early theory. Historically, de Bono certainly was the first author to write about the negative side of this system whereas many neurologists, until this day, continue to recognize but the positive effects of it. The essential negative point in self–organizing systems is that the recognition of new patterns is conditioned upon the characteristics of already existing patterns.

Bono said in his book *Serious Creativity (1996)* that when we analyze data we can only pick out the idea we already have.[12] That de Bono's insight is more than neurology is shown by the fact that Krishnamurti, Maharshi and many yogis teach us that only *total awareness*, not thought can help us understand the world intelligently.[13]

Thought or the *rational mind* is not able to recognize patterns; it can only process patterns that are already stored away in the memory surface.

The conditioning of perception by thought and by past experience was one of the arguments Krishnamurti used to show *how to overcome the limitations inherent in the thought process.* Krishnamurti showed in his writings and talks that there is unlimited intelligence and awareness not in thought but in the realm beyond thought.

In simple language, when we perceive reality, the reality we perceive never looks fresh and new, but as something al-

[12] Edward de Bono, *Serious Creativity (1992).*

[13] http://ipublica.net/ramana-maharshi/

ready known; this is so because the brain, as a matter of automatism, conditions the new information it receives upon what it already knows. Practically speaking, the patterns we perceive that can fit in existing patterns are automatically added–on to these existing patterns by the brain.

When it occurs that a new patterns reveals to be so different that it cannot be added on to any existing pattern, the brain, *instead of immediately building a new preferred pathway*, will try to bend the new pattern so much that it becomes similar to an existing pattern. Practical example: when you see an UFO landing and some extra–terrestrials leaving it, you will look at this in amazement, but later, in hindsight, you will tend to argue 'Oh yes, I guess it was just a normal airplane that I saw landing, and I was probably *hallucinating* altogether in that moment.' Your brain added the new information on to already existing information instead of forming a new pattern in the memory surface. This is how the brain, and the process of thought, works, and how this system impacts upon perception by actually per se distorting perception.

The British neurologist Herbert James Campbell gave comprehensive answers. Campbell argues that our brain has developed this kind of faulty memory surface because it was protecting human survival – while by doing it it has brought about billions of deficient thinkers! Now, how can we avoid this automatism? Krishnamurti taught that it was by practicing total attention. We can be so alert that we are aware of the brain's attempt to trick us out. A woman says:

> – I was once stolen money by a trickster. Today I
> saw a charming young trickster and stage hypno-

tist. We were flirting a moment. Then, when I looked in his eyes, it came to my mind that he just wanted to steal me money.

The new pattern was: A trickster – potential lover. The old pattern was: A trickster – thief. The new pattern did not fit in the memory surface. The pattern was: a trickster – thief. The new pattern a trickster – possible lover could not 'erase' the old pattern nor could it be added–on to it because of the contradiction thief–lover. What should we tell that lady regarding the old pattern? We saw that her brain could not erase the pattern automatically, but that some kind of input from herself was needed. I would have the following dialog with the client:

> – Please first question the validity of the old pattern! Was there not a logical fault in the old pattern as it was a generalization? A trickster who stole you money, yes or no?
>
> – Yes.
>
> – All tricksters steal money. Yes or no?
>
> – No.

Through raising her consciousness by these simple questions she could indeed have erased the old pattern; however, this is only valid for the brain, for her intellect, not for her heart: her emotions could still adhere to the old myth that all tricksters or stage hypnotists were thieves. So I tell her:

– Please engage in a new love relation in order to *disprove the validity of a single experience* that was triggering a general belief. Through a new positive experience the belief you have stored away as a result of an earlier experience can be effectively erased.

– Do you guarantee that? she asks.

– There is no guarantee in life, regarding love, I reply. If you want a guarantee for love, you kill love. When you love, go for love, not for security. Security is the death of love.

It is obvious that the second method is better than the first, because it will impact both upon the mind and the emotions of the subject.

Processed Reality

When I have a certain opinion about books, my whole attitude toward books, my handling of books, my appreciation or depreciation of books, and my habits for purchasing books are all impregnated by my opinion about books.

Whatever made me form that opinion in the first place – most of the time I will have forgotten about it anyway – is not important. The opinions I cherish have an *immediate impact* upon my perception of reality. Instead of leaving reality as it is, the brain thus processes reality by the very mechanism of perception that it uses to perceive this reality.

When I have certain religious convictions, such as the conviction that eating pork meat is bad for my health, mind, growth and attitudes, and perhaps even for my sexual behavior, my relationship with pork meat is impregnated by this conviction: in the most common case, I will make a big circle around pork meat. When I eat pork, and as a result of my convictions, I will think that I am a swine. It works like that. And in talks with others I will stress the undesired effects of pork meat. I will certainly find a great number of scientific research that proves my point of view, and thus validates my conviction that pork meat is a harmful component in the human organism. Let's get free of swinish things and habits …, you will declare, and conclude, with your habitual enthusiasm:

> – Oh folks, begin to pray for the new religion that is free of swines!

Still stronger than opinions and convictions are *beliefs*. What are beliefs? Figure beliefs as highly condensed convictions, so condensed that they have an immediate and absolute impact on our perception, an impact that is so strong and direct that we are totally unaware of it. The danger of beliefs is in fact that in most cases they are completely unconscious.

In fact, all our life circumstances are but reflections of our inner life, projected upon the interface of *real life*. From our inner state, the screen of thought and of our conscious and unconscious beliefs, energy irradiates into the universe that brings about changes and that drives us and others to various kinds of actions. Depending upon the level of integration and harmony of our inner actors, the resulting actions are effective or ineffective, constructive or destructive, harmonious or disruptive.

That is why beliefs immediately *condition* our reality. They are very important keys to understanding our personal reality, while they are really in the way of understanding our soul reality. But beliefs lose their power, and they are no more a trap to holistic perception the moment we understand their impact, when we see how powerful they actually are, and how dangerous.

When I know my beliefs, I understand my life. When I am *unconscious* of my beliefs, I am a ball for others to play with because my life is fake, as I am lacking authenticity.

Why? Because I am lacking autonomy which is a state of consciousness that is free of limiting beliefs and idiotic convictions. Living without convictions and values is the only way to be free.

Values, the big word in American power training is in fact the greatest manipulation. Because it is *but belief.* There are no values other than what I project upon the surface of my consciousness. I may setup guiding principles in my life and call them values, but what most people call values are *beliefs*.

Self–Fulfilling Prophecies

Prophecies are not only those by famous seers such as *Nostradamus*, or those contained in the Bible's Apocalypse, but also prophecies that we receive from astrologers, fortune–tellers, or numerologists. Apart from the creative flow that marks the distance between a poetically expressed prophecy and a precise time–lined event in world history, there are no popular books that report how many of Nostradamus' predictions have *not* realized in tangible reality. Thus, the proof, if there is any, would have to be corroborated by counter–proof. This is not a matter of trust or mistrust, but a matter of statistics.

Responsible and honest astrologers, numerologists and Tarot experts do not work with prophecies, and they consciously avoid being *suggestive*. As all fortune telling is but *scanning the content of consciousness* and extrapolating it onto the future, it is a volatile thing because through changing the content of my consciousness, I change my future implicitly. That is why a responsible and conscious astrologer or diviner will tell the client only the present content of their consciousness as it appears from the planetary constellations in the birth chart and all the additional vectors such as *Moon Nodes, Transits and Progressions, Part of Fortune* as well as *Lilith* and *Progressed Lilith.*

We *cannot know or predict the future* as the future is based upon the present and the present is subject to constant change and transformation. The change of the vector *Present* triggers the vector *Future* to change accordingly. Thus every prediction of the future truly is an inquiry into the content of present consciousness. Here the paranormal element comes in, which is simply telepathy. The worst prophecies are those that we use to call *self–fulfilling prophecies*, those that we give to ourselves, as a form of voicing our beliefs. For example Mister X. loudly voices at a party that he just has started a new business, and then takes a deep look in the beer glass, after which he declares:

> – Well, well, but … surely … as I know myself … and my life … all this will end like all ended before: in a complete failure …

And everybody laughs. While there was nothing, absolutely nothing to laugh about. Somebody killed himself in front of the whole audience. *Self-fulfilling prophecies are suicide.* And they have been shown to be involved also in the etiology of cancer. Recognized alternative cancer therapists Dr. Carl Simonton and Stephanie Simonton write in their book *Getting Well Again (1978/1992)* that a patient who avidly expects recovery has clearly more chances for complete healing than one who expects to die because he or she has given up any hope for recovery. They speak in either case of a *reinforcing cycle* that is put in motion through the *expectancy* they harbor and feed in their mind. They write:

Dr. O. Carl Simonton

[A]n expectation of success will often lead to success, which in turn provides evidence / that the original expectation was correct. On the other hand, an expectation of failure will often result in an unsuccessful outcome, which in turn validates the negative expectation. In both cases, the outcome created by the expectation supports the validity of the original expectation. The expectancy, whether positive or negative, gets stronger the more the cycle is repeated.[14]

---

[14] Dr. O. Carl Simonton, *Getting Well Again (1978/1992)*, pp. 80–81.

What is valid in medical science, the Simontons pursue, is also valid in education. They report in their book the following startling survey:

Dr. O. Carl Simonton

Rosenthal and his associates produced equally startling evidence on expectancy in a study conducted with children in a California public school district. A non–verbal intelligence test was administered to eighteen classrooms of elementary students at the beginning of the school year. The teachers were told that the test would predict which children were ready to bloom intellectually. Twenty percent of the students whom Rosenthal selected at random, and not on the basis of test scores, were then identified as being 'intellectual bloomers', and their teachers were told that these students could be expected to show remarkable gains during the coming year. The only difference between these students and a control group was the expectancy created in the teachers' minds. Yet when both groups of students were retested eight / months later, the randomly chosen 'bloomers' had gained in I.Q. points over the control group.[15]

Unconscious Repetition Urges

Unconscious repetition urges were first discovered by psychoanalysis. *Sigmund Freud* found a mechanism in our psyche that is quite uncanny : when we suffer a traumatic event, especially in childhood, our brain has only two possibilities:

[15] Id., pp. 81–82. The original research can be found in R. Rosenthal, *Experimenter effects in behavioral research, New York: Appleton–Century–Crofts, 1966.*

▸   shut off the computer: we turn mad; or

▸   reprogram the software: we forget all.

The brain avoids the first, as a matter of self–protection, and practices the second. While all is stored away in our memory surface, the conflictual content becomes repressed into the unconscious. And then, it happens that we attract circumstances that lead us to again and again repeat the same scenario, really or metaphorically, and this is organized by our memory surface not for bothering us, but for giving us a chance for healing the early trauma.

Alice Miller often refers to her childhood and the traumata she has suffered from a deeply narcissistic, cold, cruel and lifeless mother. But her main problem, as probably the main problem of the patients she treats in her psychiatric practice in Switzerland, is not the hurts and traumata that she or them can remember. It is those that they *cannot* remember but that are signaling their existence through the nasty fact that over and over in their lives, they are facing the same problems with people, the same problems with partners, and the same patterns in those problems; patterns that thus are similar and repetitive, or rather one pattern that manifests with a little variety.

I have tracked this pattern and found what I call an *abuse pattern* being present in many women. For example, a mother lives within a conflictual marriage where she and her partner engage in extramarital sex and pornographic parties, something that occurs in continental Europe more often than not. She has strong fears about her children, and especially the fear that her little girl could be sexually abused by a stranger. As a result of her obsessive fear, she is suspicious about her babysitter, as he is a male, and she is kind of convinced that all males want to abuse once in a while, just to prove themselves they are males. After further talks, I invariably found with such clients that they had been abused in their younger years or during their girlhood by either their father or stepfather, their grandfather, an uncle, an older brother, a cousin, or a boyfriend when they were dating for the first time.

Thus, I did not need to read Alice Miller to know about that specific pattern. I had enough crying mothers in front of me, when over a cup of coffee they told me about what they called their 'problem'.

And in a case that particularly touched me, I was dumbfounded to see how inescapable the fate seems to be that unconscious repetition urges bring about. When I was seven years old, I fell in love with a neighbor girl, Ursula.

Ursula was the daughter of a policeman who was working with the French military, the former occupation force in our town. He was thus a horse–top policeman, called in French, a *cavalier*. But he was not a gentleman toward his daughter, because he was whipping her regularly for punishment. And that girl suffered terribly from the sadism of her father and our relationship was rendered impossible by that sadist and equally by the girl's very suspicious and neurotic mother, to a point that she simply was forbidden to ride on the bike with me. She was never allowed to leave the house when I came to pick her up.

After almost twenty years I met her again, by chance, in a little bistro in our town. And she told me the following story:

Ursula P.

I have suffered terribly from men in my life. First my father and then my husband. You know what my father did to me, but you don't know what my husband did. He raped me constantly and was beating me, so that I asked for the divorce. We were divorced and after the divorce, he broke in my apartment and raped me again. I had to call the police but they said they could not really protect me.

Unconscious repetition urge means that destiny wanted Ursula get beyond her affliction and once for all *solve her victim condition*, a problem of co–fusion, of co–dependence puzzled up with hate–love feelings toward her father. You may think Ursula will get a gun and shoot down the next guy who attempts to take advantage of her. Yet that is not what usually happens in life. That's perhaps the movies, but not real life. And it's no solution because the abuse pattern is within Ursula, not without. And it can't be healed through violence, but only through consciousness.

It's only possible if Ursula can regress again in her childhood, during medical hypnosis or any other method that uses hypnosis implicitly, or if Ursula can play it out in a psycho-drama with a male who in some way stands for all those who have abused her in the past. And through that game–like role play, Ursula could observe her reaction and her feelings and see what exactly in her attracts men that violate her integrity. When Ursula was seven years old, she could not do that work and her brain had to react with a trauma response. But with twenty–seven that archaic reaction of the brain is not any more for Ursula's best and she has to learn alternatives in behavior and regarding her expectations so as to attract men that care for her, love her and see the beauty in her.

The tragedy in Ursula's life and the lives of so many others who have had traumatic childhoods is that at least once they met their savior, but were not allowed to develop the relationship. I was for Ursula that person, that savior, the one who unconditionally loved and understood her, a boy of her age. Many dreams that I received in my childhood about her and me confirmed that.

The tragedy was that our love was impossible – rendered impossible by *exactly the violators that traumatized her entire life*. Her parents.

Spiritual Pitfalls

> The recognition of the secondary nature of the personality of whatever deity is worshipped is characteristic of most of the traditions of the world. In Christianity, Mohammedanism, and Judaism, however, the personality of the divinity is taught to be final – which makes it comparatively difficult for the members of these communions to understand how one may go beyond the limitations of their own anthropomorphic divinity. The result has been, on the one hand, a general obfuscation of the symbols, and on the other, a god–ridden bigotry such is unmatched elsewhere in the history of religion. For a discussion of the possible origin of this aberration, see Sigmund Freud, Moses and Monotheism, 1939.
>
> – JOSEPH CAMPBELL, THE HERO WITH A THOUSAND FACES, NEW YORK: PRINCETON UNIVERSITY PRESS, 1949, THIRD PRINTING, 1973, PP. 258, 259, NOTE 5.

Churches

Among spiritual sense givers churches are at the first place because they are considering themselves as *superconscious organizations* established for man's spiritual welfare – while in truth they are representations of our inner shadow, the black man that we bear inside, the part of us that is not light, not conscious, and thus in a *magic condition*, and as a result subject of, and subjected to, *myths and mythologies.*

Churches and their like institutions in other religions have the nasty habit to interfere in people's lives like your mother–in–law, telling you what you ought to do, and what you ought not to. As if you were a baby or a psychotic, or a psychotic baby. It's a fact that churches and other so–called *spiritual organizations* exert power over people that subject themselves to them as their believers. Apart from the interesting word play that this represents when we think of what beliefs are and how devastating they are for any success in life, we may understand what we can expect from churches – and what we *cannot* expect from them.

In Singapore, the Christian churches have a spicy note that distinguishes them from Christian churches in the West: when the time of the mass approaches, the yard is filled with shiny new cars, predominantly Mercedes and BMW, Jaguar and Rolls–Royce, and inside the building the walls are covered with big and golden panels that cite in detail who has given which contribution to the church's monetary fund. The amounts range from several thousand Singapore dollars to several hundred thousand Singapore dollars each. When I asked a Christian Singapore Chinese what he thought about that, he openly laughed and declared:

Christian Singapore Chinese

But Christian churches in Singapore have nothing to do with the Christian dogma. They are prime meeting places for business people to get

> to know each other and to talk business. That is
> why we go to Church!

And when you join a mass in Geneva's Cathedral on a Sunday morning, you will hear how spicy Swiss Calvinism can be out of the mouth of a *sadist* and world–hater that declares all pleasure as 'sin' and the children's carousel in front of the Cathedral an 'invention of the devil'.

Human theatre? I agree. But what the hell has it to do with spirituality? To split life in a spiritual and a non–spiritual part per se destroys any chance to get beyond the soup of mass thinking. The way to a spiritual life simply, and importantly, begins with questioning our beliefs, and all the rest of the human soup that preaches mediocrity, fatality and misery as the human condition.

The true way to spirituality consists in learning to say *No*, and again. Until something happens that was not expected and that you might call *bliss*. The Baby Jesus was a fist in the face of all churches! And a prisoner incarcerated for loving a child is a fist in the face of all so–called human justice.

Sects

It is a tragic irony that churches are trying to distance themselves from sects. They do this after they saw that sects simply were more radical, while they are for the most part based upon exactly the same principles as churches.

When I applied for a position with the *European Parliament's Administration* in Luxembourg, I was invited to participate in a nationwide competition in which eight hundred

German lawyers participated. The subject of one of the written tests, guess it, was sects. At the time, in 1983, sects had become a European problem, as not only the member states of the EU were suffering from the sect problem, but the European Union as a whole tried to get hold of the 'spiritual epidemics', so to say, by giving out guidelines to all the ministries of education of all member states about how to handle the sect problem.

What had been my recommendations? I in fact recommended to not treat the symptoms but cure the disease. What was the disease? A spiritual vacuum in young people. And I had seen how it happened with a friend of mine who was a blooming youth, artist and teacher, before he entered that sect in France, and after they had brainwashed and force–married him in that sect, he was a decrepit elder with a rigid, judgmental mindset. And that sect was named *The Church of Enlightenment.*

They obviously *and for well–founded reasons* had avoided to name the organization a sect in order to circumvent the national and supranational regulations against sects. From the basic paradigm, the life denial, the dogmatic approach, the repressive attitudes toward children, with their resulting harsh beatings, the Draconian restrictions on lifestyle, diet and sexual behavior and the arrogant preaching of so–called truth 'in the name of Jesus Christ', they were exactly behaving like most churches. And the danger for modern society comes equally from both churches and sects, because it's only the label in which they differ.

Gurus

And there are those who think they are especially modest and virtuous. They do not go to churches because they find that old-fashioned, and they do not join sects because they do not want to restrict their lifestyle. Thus, they travel to India to see Sai Baba or any other guru with a certain reputation. And then they come back with longer hair, dirty clothes and an enlightened mind.

The guru and the disciple engage in a *shared form of corruption* and they are both responsible for it, not only one of them. They both play theatre, not only the guru. They both share in the same comedy, or tragedy, as you wish to see it. They are actors on the same stage. And their credo is: you have to follow a better one so that you will become better. You have to follow a higher one so that you become higher. You have to follow a more intelligent one so that you become more intelligent. You have to follow an humbler one so that you become more humble. You have to follow a famous one so that one day you will be famous. And so on.

Guruism is one of many outflows of the *hero paradigm* that is in turn a direct result of the patriarchal rut with its rigid senior–junior hierarchy among males, and even among females, but stronger rooted among males.[16] Gurus, not those who are *meta-teachers* by living their truth, such as Krishnamurti, but *self-declared gurus* and especially those who call themselves 'spiritual teachers' are professing to know better than their disciples how the latter should live their lives.

---

[16] See Pierre F. Walter, *The Hero Culture*, Audiobook (2010).

Where they take this superiority from remains occult, and is not explainable simply because in matters of our individual quest for truth, there is no hierarchy, absolutely no hierarchy among humans.

This is simply so. We are called upon as individuals to find our personal reality, as an intimate quest, a search for our own *Holy Grail* that can be found only in our heart, and not in the bosom of any guru.

Saviors

Every religion cherishes a savior, some kind of super–human that is put as the living ideal, the first–class vintage, so to say, the best of the best in terms of human perfection – or whatever that might be. And that is exactly where the problem is resulting from. Saviors are mythical figures, full of mystery and disdain, it seems, for so–called 'ordinary reality'. They are nice as actors on the stage of fairy tales. But they are not nice when taken as ideal humans, as targets for projecting our wishes to be better than we are. Because in this quality, they are truly destructive for our growth.

Saviors are supposed to live special lives, lives of magic and wonder, lives that we all would like to live. But when we look and compare, for example historical facts and feats from the real lives of Jesus of Nazareth or Gautama Buddha, we see that there is really a large gap, to say the least, between what we can find was their real life, and what later was made out of that life and out of that person.

Jesus and Buddha were later declared to be cosmic masterminds. Gee. Oh. Dee. [17]

What is Gee Oh Dee?

A new song? An old soup? The name of a famous actress? No. The name of that super–savior mastermind, the big brother robot that is supposed to be the lonely baboon, the biggest boss or the most original hacker in our universe. A story for youngsters – at best.

All savior stories are hero stories. Food not for thought, but for your inner child. [18] When you are conscious of the damage these kindergarten stories do and have done in the course of humanity, you can prevent that the damage is going to affect you, and you can avoid to fall in the savior–trap, as a result of a *narcissistic fixation*, in becoming the savior for your mother, your father, your brother, your sister, your spouse or your child. Not only mental hospitals are full of saviors and Jesus Christs, but also most families.

Françoise Dolto, in a workshop for child therapy back in 1988 reports the case of a young boy suffering from a *priapus*, a painful long–term erection of his penis that lasted for months. The father, a bank director, was in high sorrow about what he called the 'indecent condition' of his child and took the boy to Françoise Dolto's famous psychoanalytic practice in Paris. [19]

---

[17] http://ipublica.net/jesus-of-nazareth/

[18] http://ipublica.net/inner-selves/

[19] http://ipublica.net/francoise-dolto/

Dolto was able to cure the boy from the long–term erection of his penis, but two weeks after the successful termination of the cure, the mother of the boy called Dolto and said her husband had died from a heart attack.

The boy had been the savior of his father and as long as he was the suffering agent, the father could keep the balance in an otherwise unbalanced life. When the boy was cured, the father's crutches were taken away and he fell struck dead.

Ideological Pitfalls

Today, the propaganda machine of *postmodern international consumerism* is the result of more than a millennium of knowledge prohibition, spiritual manipulation and systematically bred life–hate. It is the newest and the most fashionable of our present–day sociopolitical ideologies.

Consumerism blindfolds the masses surely in a sweeter way than the Church's brutal knowledge prohibition that was enforced by the Inquisition and endless witchhunts.[20] The sweetness and big promise of freedom as an integral part of consumer culture guarantees much higher effectiveness than coercion or brute force in repressing the original love wishes of the populace.

This is so because in fact subtle media–based manipulation is used to innocuously replacing emotional and sexual longings by material longings for acquiring and possessing consumer goods. And when looking at it in a superficial way, I gain freedom when I exchange a part of my money in the bank with a nicely designed and smoothly running sports car, plasma television or computer notebook. I gain creative freedom, can move around in a splendid way, comfortably, and can get a self–esteem boost through the admiration I receive from others for being an XY–Limousine owner or a VZ–Notebook owner. Besides that, I can write, compose, draw and publish my media productions in fully using the creative possibilities of my notebook.

---

[20] http://ipublica.net/perversion/#Inquisition

This superficial observation however veils the fact that the overwhelming majority of limousine and notebook owners are *not more substantially creative* after buying these goods than they were before. Or, put differently, the truth is that my real freedom is not that I have money in the bank that allows me to buy or not buy consumer goods. My real freedom is to be able to live without working for anybody, without being a slave for eight hours a day, forty hours a week. By the same token, my real freedom is my urge to be creative, constantly creative, and it makes no substantial difference if I use a notebook or write by hand on a simple sheet of paper, else paint on a canvas, or improvise on the piano.

My real freedom thus is my spiritual drive or soul's desire to surpass my mere physical human condition and express my ideas, or create art.

When you take a deeper look, you see that the masses are cheated twice through the promises of consumerism. They for the most part do not have enough money in the bank, or property, or company shares allowing them to live a meaningful existence without working for somebody. Thus, what indeed most people need and desire is freedom!

Consumer culture promises this freedom, but let us see what it boils down to. For acquiring the goods that will grant me some form of creative freedom, I need money. For acquiring the money that I need to buy these goods, I need to work, and *work more than usual*, because I need a surplus of money, a lot more than the amount I anyway need for food, clothes and shelter, or the education of my children. How to get this amount of surplus money?

Through effort, increased effort and still more increased effort. Thus, in order to *expand myself more* within consumer culture, I in fact need to *curb myself more.* For every dollar of surplus money, I need to work relatively harder than for the same dollar of money covering my basic human needs for food and shelter.

Of course, this reality is blinded out by publicity, and one essential task of publicity is precisely to blindfold the consumer, suggesting that the acquisition of goods is smooth and easy, using consumer credit as the ultimate backdoor for climbing on the bandwagon. However, it has been shown by leading financial consultants that the consumer credit is the single most destructive form of credit there is in the economy. This is so because the *consumer credit*, contrary to the business credit, is not backed up by an increase in productivity, but in the contrary needs a constant almost super–human effort to produce the surplus of financial resources needed to pay back the credit. It is a time bomb!

This is so much the more embarrassing when the duration of the credit surpasses the average life–span of the consumer good. For example, when my computer notebook is trash after two years because of the swindling progress in IT technology, and I need four years of credit duration to finance it, I will use two years of my life to pay for something that I do not use any more and that does not give me any more freedom or creativity value. Of course, you may still use your notebook, but you are highly incited to sell it for a very low price and buy a new model using another consumer credit.

This is how in very credit–intensive consumer cultures such as the United States, people who seem well–to–do on first sight, actually are often caught in a net of credits that, if the slightest event happens that disturbs the credit pay-back–cycle, the card house crashes and people who were enjoying life yesterday, today plan to suicide themselves.

It is not a Marxist idea, then, to say that this system incarcerates the ignorant masses in pretty much the same false beliefs than previously the religious caste did with their endless taboos. Marx and Engels have brilliantly analyzed the destructive effects of capitalism, but acting on these insights brought about governmental regulation, prohibition and coercion, unfreedom, persecution and even torture and murder. And all this justified by the initial intent to prevent the masses from indebting themselves destructively.

That's how it goes. These policies were wrong and ineffective because they disregarded the basic human need for *distinction*, and the readiness of human beings to give sustained effort, and even sacrifice themselves for a higher quality of life, a higher social status, academic or scientific distinction, opportunity for travel, more popularity or a greater circle of friends and acquaintances. Clearly, these values are not commercial and what the communist ideologies have overlooked is that the human being does not per se strive for money or for accumulating money or other riches.

What people strive for is the creative freedom that wealth brings, and they do so with very good reasons, with the main reason namely that this freedom is real freedom and not the fake freedom of consumerism. Modern culture has no idea of how to live a happy life. It replaces true happiness with fake–values that suggest consumer satiation being the ultimate enjoyment in life.

> 'I have a new car, refrigerator and air–condition, a home theater and the walls in my garage covered with books. I am a well–red and cultured person. I work hard and go to the gym in my free time. I am married with a wife and three children. My wife works. My children go to school. I am a happy citizen. I have a family. I have values. I have convictions. I have possessions. I have.'

Possessions–based lifestyle kills every form of culture. And when you look at modern life you realize that it's not a culture, but a *fake–culture*, that it's not based upon values, but upon *fake–values*, and that the people on the stage are not humans, but marionettes.

Postmodern international consumer culture is based upon the genocide of countless tribal populations who *really* knew what happiness is about and who lived happy lives – until they were massacred by value–based and principle–ridden modern citizens.

Emotional Pitfalls

'A random telephone survey of 800 American adults in September 1996 found that 74 percent – virtually three out of four citizens – believe that the U.S. government regularly engages in conspirational and clandestine operations.'

ROBERT A. WILSON, EVERYTHING IS UNDER CONTROL: CONSPIRACIES, CULTS AND COVER–UPS, NEW YORK: HARPER & ROW (HARPER–RESOURCE), 1998.

What did Gandhi mean when he said that spiritual training should be *educating the heart?* Gandhi was talking about raising *emotional intelligence* and holistic thinking. *Worldwide Democracy*, as we all know, moves rather in the opposite direction.

We will always have secret services, conspiracies and persecutions as long as we uphold the paranoid view that there is a *greater force* that shapes our individual destinies instead of realizing that we are *the only makers of our personal universe.*

Countless individuals throughout human history have demonstrated that they were able to shape their destinies according to their own intrinsic life paradigm and soul values, refusing to subordinate their vision under shallow mainstream convictions.

Worldwide Democracy is based upon the exact opposite vision of the human being, namely on the myth that *total consumption* is what basically makes happy living. This goal, evidently serving economic interests, is largely veiled by a moralistic and fundamentalist cover paradigm and by a bulk of *myths*. The cover paradigm, which is one of projection and persecution, is generally hidden to mainstream consumers.

The veil however can be lifted quite easily by those with an inquisitive and critical mind. The information, while it is filtered by mainstream media, is easily available through alternative presses and the Internet. But as it does not fit in the rosy foam of glorious consumerism, thus after filtering, what remains in the mainstream media are the myths, and the projections.

The main targets of the strategy of repression–and–projection are the *Muslims* and the *Pedophiles*; both groups, strategically demonized in public with a growing emphasis on their *difference*, are supposed to embody the evil that is believed to erode the happy consumer world with its asexual and emotionally castrated children that, consequently, need to be strongly protected and meticulously supervised. This is why *child protection* is actually an over–arching myth that serves as an ideological goal and polemics maker just in the same way as the racial purification theories of an Adolf Hitler or the intellectual purification theories of a Pol Pot.

What stands behind this new form of fascism, that for this time in history truly is worldwide, as it is sponsored by the publishing multimedia giants, is a basic *denial of complexity*, which has been proven by historians, and among them especially Jacob Burckhardt, as one of the roots of fascism.[21]

This can easily be made out by an intelligent observer, when following up the daily news on the subject of Islam and what it pretendedly is up to, the wars in Iraq and Afghanistan, and how they are justified, the new impending war with Iran, and what is advanced in public by the United States government to justify it, and the blunt ignorance and one-sided polemics that stares out of any media coverage on the subject of adult-child erotic relations.

It is not difficult to see the obvious parallels between the present scapegoat groups and the historic ones. Even today, the old persecutions have not ceased either. Anti-Semitism is on the rise again, and that despite the protection that the state of Israel enjoys by the United States of America and other Western powers. The stress when analyzing fascism should perhaps not be put so much on the *objects* of the current or past persecutions, but on the *general climate* that leads to intolerance and persecution. As to this general climate, I am certainly not alone in saying that we are again in an era of political and social intolerance, of irrationality, of blunt media manipulation and of persecution. And what I am saying here is essentially that the new salvational construct that is put in the formula *worldwide democracy* is actually at the basis

___

[21] http://ipublica.net/complexity/

of the new danger to true humanity, as it serves as an easy eye–catcher and an attractive packaging device. It's truly a Pandora box. And contained in it, there is a time–bomb that ticks.

The myths I am talking about here are observable phenomena, not only theorems, and have a rather widespread if not devastating influence upon the non–reflective and consumption–prone mass mind.

And when this is true for adults, how much more children are affected by this ultimate postmodern form of mass hypnosis!

Out of a large number of myths, I will select a few and shortly present them in this last part of the theoretical first part of the study.

THE MYTHS OF WORLDWIDE DEMOCRACY

The Myth of Child Protection

Many parents who think they are *modern and generous* to their children are in reality consume–training their children and molding them into co–dependent partners.[22] Unconsciously such parents act as the long arm of political systems and ideologies subtly hypnotizing their children with the concepts they have themselves been fed with. It is for this reason revolutionary, if not considered subversive, to rear children in truth and autonomy. For such kind of education is not compatible with the Oedipal–paranoid worldview that mainstream education is based upon.[23] To raise children responsibly does surely not mean to charge them with a burden of responsibility that they cannot meet. *However, the contrary is perhaps worse.*

To infantilize children, discard them out of real life, institutionalize them into plastic worlds of crap and lies, and *degrade them into obligatory play* is part of the tactics of Oedipal confusion that justifies its utterly manipulative attitude with the claim it was serving to protect the child. *Oedipal confusion* brings about highly adapted standard citizens that are deeply disloyal! In fact, the reigning Oedipal mainstream culture is a *community of secret anarchists* that obediently say their credo, but

---

[22] http://ipublica.net/co-dependence/

[23] http://ipublica.net/oedipal-culture/

silently sabotage the very content of it. By contrast, education toward autonomy is based upon recognizing the existence of *soul values* and the *unique truth* of every single child, also and especially if this individual truth is *contrary* to the reigning sociopolitical ideologies.

It is disturbing today's global consumer culture that the child be a *complete human* and thus a *sexual being* from birth, and that, as a result, children own a birthright to have their emotions and sexual feelings respected.

Françoise Dolto, the late French child therapist, wrote in her book *La Cause des Enfants (1985)* that it scandalizes most parents that a child be their equal and that, therefore, most parents raise their children as formerly princes ruled their kingdom.

Why this is so is obvious: a body–conscious child is not an easy consumer of compensatory toys and a thousand devices artificially created by international consumer reality and that are after all but cultural trash.

For those who contradict this view, I recall that the repression of the child's sexuality has exactly started with the onset of the Western industrial bourgeoisies, toward the end of the 17th century, and not, as many researchers wrongly believe, with the beginning of patriarchy. See, for example Françoise Dolto, *La Cause des Enfants (1985)* who reports, citing Ariès, about the childhood of French King Louis XIII:

Françoise Dolto

Until he was six years old, adults behaved with the prince in a perverse way: they played with his penis, allowed him to play with their genitals and to sleep

> with them and play 'the little devil' with them. All this was allowed. But suddenly when he was six years old, they dressed him like an adult and he had to follow the royal etiquette (citing Ariès, L'Enfant et la vie familiale sous l'Ancien Régime, p. 145). Despite the trauma that could follow, he had nonetheless kept something essential since, during the first years of his life, he could live his sexuality with other adults than his parents. He had here more chance in spite of the precocious adult clothing they put him in. His example is only valid for the rich classes. However, in other levels of society, how could a child of that time repress his incestuous desire and sublimate it?[24]

Historical studies about child rearing practices in Europe stress the fact that still in the Renaissance, the sexuality of the child was not interfered with. Back in the Middle–Ages, apart from orthodox Christian circles, it was completely free.[25]

I would like to introduce here a useful dichotomy coined by the psychoanalyst Erich Fromm.[26] He created a simple metaphor calling current consumer society a state of *to have*, and original unspoiled being, a state of *to be*. Our original body pleasure and natural psychosomatic connection between body and mind is the state Fromm called *To Be*. Consumerist industrialization replaced that condition by *To Have*, a state of affairs where body and mind are split and the mind

---

[24] See Françoise Dolto, *La Cause des Enfants (1985)*, pp. 28, 29 (Translation mine).

[25] See, for example, Susanne Cho, *Kindheit und Sexualität im Wandel der Kulturgeschichte (1983)* and Floyd M. Martinson, *The Sex Education of Young Children (1981)*, 51.

[26] http://ipublica.net/erich-fromm/

acting, most of the time, against the body. This state of *To Have* is the primary condition for consumer society to function because if people firmly decided to stay with *To Be*, our marketing system would not work.

It's working because people, already in early childhood, are *conditioned away from the body* and into the mind, something our schools know to do brilliantly and which is emosexual castration combined with intellectual hypertrophy. In good English, these kids talk like university professors when invited at a birthday party, but their emotions and their genitals are dried out. They have turned sadistic in their general mindset, and their high–pitched voices express their mix of subordination combined with inner revolt and growing violence.

Have you ever met an *emotionally and sexually sane* child, a child who is sexually active? Such a child has a dark–pitched and slightly smoky voice!

Consumer culture is founded not on pleasure, *but on ersatz pleasure*. Ersatz pleasure is the pleasure that replaces original body pleasure; thus first of all the industrial toy. While the self–made toy still has some connection with the body, the industrially produced toy is completely alien to the child's body.

Typically this toy – which in the meantime is produced by a gigantic global industry – consists of materials not akin to the human body, such as plastic or metal. Both plastic and metal are cold and rigid while the body is warm and pliable. Unconsciously children are conditioned upon the characteristics of the toys they is playing with.

– *Be plastic!* translates into *Be without true feelings and artificial!*

– *Be metal!* translates into *Be hard and mechanical!*

This is how the child is molded upon the values of the culture he is born into. In addition, consumer education uses techniques of confusion as educational methods to gradually alienate the child from their own truth – which is their body continuum. The child namely thinks from the body toward the mind, and thus inductively, while the conditioned adult thinks from the mind toward the body, and thus deductively.

This means that the child's truth is defined and experienced as the truth of their body. Every truth that disregards this body or tries to set it aside will not be regarded by the child as truth. It is for this reason that children cannot comprehend moralistic educational concepts since those concepts *starve the body and hypertrophy the intellect*. The consequence are lifelong giant water–headed babies in the form of adults who have never made the cut with their childhood, remaining emotionally and sexually immature. *True virgins*. While life has not made us to remain virgins, but to leave virginity and grow into loving copulation.

The fundamental conditioning of man is accomplished at the age of six, which is since Freud an established assumption in psychoanalysis. What comes later is only polish. The Oedipal confusion cheats about this truth. It creates a confused mind within an immature and rigid nonsexual body that has lost its natural intelligence. This is neurosis programmed into culture! Oedipal confusion plays the game of eternal maternity until the baby is far older than thirty!

It loves naive mother dependence and shuns and mistreats children who are precociously mature.[27] It blows the child care industry up to a gigantic worldwide business with children as their products!

Children who resist the cultural castration and maintain their natural capacity for sexual love and sensual pleasure are put in the corner and labeled as *sexualized and delinquent*. If they still dare to play their own game, the child psychiatrist is ready to interfere and to issue a certificate which will mark the social death blow: *schizophrenic* or *epileptic*.

The Myth of Civilization

Many religions have tried to force peace upon man by dogma, prohibitions and punishment. Clerical and worldly forces have imprisoned humanity in a set of tight rules, laws and prescriptions that have had only one result: to render man a violent beast full of contempt, rebellion, strife, falseness and turmoil. To get out of this net of obligations and the feeling of oppression that goes along with it, man is caught in an endless pursuit of pleasure.

To make it worse, through the split in man's mental and emotional setup as a result of the schizoid dualism that judging our emotions in good and bad ones brings about, our psyche is divided in a conscious or official part and an unconscious or unofficial one. Through the process of so–called *civilization* and primarily the school system with its mass indoctrination and the disregard of the individual as a unique

---

[27] http://ipublica.net/emotional-abuse/

soul–being, humanity has in fact devoluted since the great Minoan and other pre–patriarchal cultures of Antiquity.

In fact, evolution has made its way only in the tiny range of technological advancement while in all other areas of life, we are today more barbarian than five thousand years ago.

Therefore, the solution for world peace is entirely different from what clerical and worldly powers have ever taught us. Truly, only those who were considered as heretics, saints or prophets have told the truth. Buddha, when he was alive, found truth by human struggle and suffering, while after his death his teaching was perverted into its exact contrary.

Through levitating the man Buddha into a god–like tower of virtue, the applicability of his teachings for us was impeded, if not rendered totally vain.

The Myth of Control

In killing the *pleasure function* and submitting it to group supervision and control, the human race has signed a contract with the devil, after having created this devil as a split self that controls the controller.[28] Most of us are dulled and pacified into aloofness, and our once critical sense has been castrated and sanitized, first through the emotional death we suffered in childhood, second through the intellectual and neurotic overdrive we are in, as adults, as a compensation for the connectedness we lost, and third through the constant mass media manipulation we are too weak or too lazy to resist.

---

[28] http://ipublica.net/pleasure-function/

It is a deep fatal error to think that this was a *modern* phenomenon.

The analysis of human evolution shows that the present worldwide murder culture has its roots in our five thousand years of patriarchal history. In fact, it is ignorant to believe anything in nature or in the human–created world could come about in a vacuum. The present multi–faceted and institutionalized murders are based upon a *murder tradition* that goes back to the *Code of Hammurabi*, or what Wilhelm Reich[29] called *The First Human No* to the endless flow of life, represented by the natural ebb–and–flow of pleasure.[30] It is equally naïve and ignorant to believe that the present catastrophic state of affairs could have come about through any specific religion or ideology.

While still decades ago, the human masses were so ignorant to believe that most ideologies were necessary or even god–given, many today start to question this. But instead of seeing the failure of *all ideologies* for the advancement of humanity, they blame particular ideologies, such as Islam, while upholding others, more akin to their race or mindset.

The Bible is very explicit in favoring the in–group and excluding the out–group, and murder was not only permitted but *even ordained* by Yahweh, the cultural divinity, when there was a need to advance in one's business through domination and the ruthless holocaust of those that were naturally opposing such dominion.

---

[29] http://ipublica.net/wilhelm-reich/

[30] See Wilhelm Reich, *Children of the Future (1955)*.

Today's short—sighted Western credo is that by and large Islamic culture was to blame for the terrible disorder in the world. This assumption overlooks that Islam shares with Christianity and Judaism the *same base paradigm and murderous ideology* that promises human advancement based upon the rape and repression of nature, oligarchic control and the hypertrophy of *yang* to the detriment of *yin*. This terrible lie, that is by itself the root of murder, has been paid with innumerable victims, in the past, and today, and it has caused humanity to retrograde in its evolution.

The Myth of Culture

Freud reasoned that culture was based upon the sublimation of our instincts. While Freud clearly said that sublimation is not to be equated with repression, at the end of the day the difference between sublimation and repression seems minimal.[31]

Sigmund Freud meant that while he was in favor of children living freely their sexuality, he thought that for cultural reasons, medical and psychiatric experts had to accept the cultural choice of the repression of the child's early sexuality, limiting their professional role to healing the neuroses and psychoses that result from this choice.[32] A deeper look reveals that it is nothing less than an act of castration to forbid the child his or her own sexuality. This is a form of parental or

---

[31] http://ipublica.net/sigmund-freud/
http://ipublica.net/repression/

[32] http://childsexuality.net

educational child mutilation, a form of societal child rape, if our hypocrite culture considers it as such or not.

Since Havelock Ellis it is clear that all sexual deviations and neuroses are born out of the repression of children's and adolescents' healthy sexuality.[33] If parents, as a consequence of their own sex–denying upbringing, are inhibited from talking openly with their children about sex, they should at least be able to psychologically support their children by *adopting a permissive and non–obtrusive attitude* regarding their children's intimate lives.

It is a relict of patriarchal tradition that boys and girls are treated as two different species with regard to their sexual urges and behavior. Gender impregnation that is too early and too strong will suppress certain valuable characteristics in children that are attributed to the opposite sex, as for example tenderness, caring behavior, altruism, patience with men and activity, healthy egoism and competitive thinking or impatience with women.

Havelock Ellis found that the early repression of sexuality in girls was a major factor in female frigidity. The feminist view underlines that the problem is not the repression of basic drives but the general oppression of women and children. Who can be interested in perpetuating sexual dysfunctions in both sexes as a result of sexual repression during childhood and adolescence?

Who can be interested in rising sexual deviance, suicide rates and rape? Who wants to favor the escalation of vio-

---

[33] http://ipublica.net/havelock-ellis/

lence, racism, war and destruction? For all this is the price we have to pay for maintaining the clean, pure and asexual façade behind which we hide all the negative secondary impulses which come up as a result of repressing the natural sexual function.

It is not surprising that after centuries of sexual repression and the distortion of the knowledge about natural life functions now society needs scientific corroboration of the most banal realities of life. But after all, it's absurd. Experience shows that people with natural attitudes toward sexuality will also be inclined to accept new permissive forms of education whereas people with sexual inhibitions and moralistic concepts tend to be suspicious of new and non–authoritarian concepts of education.[34]

So–called child sexual abuse is a fake cause, a propagandistic cover–up of the *real abuse* in our culture, which is rampant parent–child co–dependence, which constitutes emotional abuse, and besides, physical abuse.[35] Our mass media debates regarding children's alleged sexual innocence are but fights about words; all concern about trauma through early sexual experiences are but projections of adults' own orgasmic fears and armoring against natural biological functions.

Anna Freud's research on war children in London during World War II provided striking counter–evidence to the *fake* trauma theories of today's mainstream abuse culture; children are *not* traumatized by sex, and not even by bombs fal-

---

[34] http://ipublica.net/permissive-education/

[35] http://child-sexual-abuse.com

ling all around of them in wars and civil wars. They are only when their *parents* are bundles of walking paranoia and when they thus have been *conditioned* to be apprehensive to all and everything in life. Natural children are fearless.[36]

The most devastating effects in adult–child sexual encounters do not result from sex but from fear and panic associated with engaging in a tabooed and not coded form of conduct.[37] An analogy to this situation can be seen in the psychological reasons for *drowning accidents.* While infants can swim without having learnt swimming, older children and adults lost this ability because of the fear associated with drowning. Research has shown that many people who died through drowning could have been saved if they had received proper psychological training to cope with panic.

Adults' fear of water is irrational in much the same way as is *orgasmic fear.* Water, in the subconscious, is being associated with emotions and sexuality.

Society is for a large part responsible for the killing of children in chaotic sexual encounters because of its refusal to *code* certain forms of behavior. This is a *collective form of irresponsibility* that hits society at large in much the same way, or even more, than the individual perpetrator. Moral wars and hysteria cannot replace responsible laws and rules of con-

---

[36] http://ipublica.net/anna-freud/

[37] See the early research results on the matter by Bender & Blau, *The Reaction of Children to Sexual Relations with Adults,* American J. of Orthopsychiatry 7 (1937), 500-518.

duct; in the contrary, they tend to prevent or disable such rules.

This is one of the most obvious reasons why *pedoemotions* and the whole spectrum of sexual behavior between adults and minors needs to be coded socially.[38]

A social code – which is much more than a legal statute in that it encompasses certain forms of conduct that are socially acceptable – is the only way to maintain culture while the present irresponsible attitude produces chaos, confusion, insecurity and, at worst, a new form of civil war.

It has been shown by a great amount of research that there is a functional link between the repression of the human sexual drive and the upsurge of violence. It is first of all the *repression of the child's natural sexual function* and the social disapproval of tactile pleasure for certain age groups that prepares the ground for societal violence.[39]

Thus the cultural choice that Freud wanted to respect and preserve was a culture not founded upon nature, but upon *perverted* nature. And that is why all the problems that culturally today we are dealing with, first of all the problem of rampant domestic, social and structural violence, are our own creation, and not at all an outcome of any fault in the original human setup. It's our collective denial to assume responsibility for our emotions, and our sexual function, that

---

[38] http://pedoemotions.com

[39] See, for example, the research by James W. Prescott, Ashley Montagu, Herbert James Campbell, Michel Odent, Frederick Leboyer, and others, in the Bibliography annexed to this essay.

among other factors are the most obvious pitfalls in our constant drawbacks and individual and social catastrophes.

The Myth of Education

Striving for autonomy is an inherent component in every young life. Therefore hyper–protective education *clearly is a form of child abuse* because it smashes children's natural autonomy through emosexual deprivation. *Mainstream education sacrifices the child–as–a–person for bringing about the child–as–a–consumer.* I call this education *death education* since it is based upon the emosexual murder of children in order to subvert them into consumer robots. To achieve this, mainstream education uses what I call braincut to castrate children emotionally and sexually.[40]

Modern society acts here much after the example of the Church. The Church, while paying lip service to love, destroyed love by instilling in their believers an horrible fear of pleasure and by punishing, through the Inquisition, free unregulated love in every possible way, including putting people to death by persecution, torture and planned murder and genocide.

Modern society castrates the child emotionally through a hypertrophy of the left brain hemisphere and logical thinking, while downplaying, circumventing and outright neglecting the development of the qualities of the right brain hemisphere, such as creative intuitions, associative thinking, systemic thinking, fantasy and creativity.

---

[40] http://emosexuality.com

The Myth of Morality

There is no god, no savior and no punishment. There are no wrong acts, nor right acts. There is karma only, feedback given by the universe. By observing that feedback and recognizing its nature, positive or negative, I can evaluate the nature of my actions. There is no other way. You can't do that by thinking about your behavior. Thought is circular and inbound within my own continuum. I cannot abstract from my thought and become an observer–thinker, despite the fact that great sages such as Krishnamurti told us we could develop this ability. Let's assume I have not reached that stage of development and thus am still caught in the ego–based structure. Then I have the option to observe the nature of my actions by evaluating the feedback they create in the universe.

In being careful and observing what happens around you before you take any major action, you can avoid fatal mistakes and setbacks and act in accordance with the steering power of the universe. This power is of a *higher intelligence*, and considers not only your actions but the actions of all other humans, of all other beings, and even the actions of natural forces. How does a particular action you are going to take fit in the universe? What kind of waves will it create? What kind of responses will it trigger? All this can be evaluated before the action is taken. And the I Ching has been created exactly to assist us in that quest.[41]

---

[41] http://ipublica.net/i-ching/

Once you understand this, you will agree that to take blind actions is a foolish thing. And yet, most people, especially in the modern world, take blind actions all the time, and even think that it was normal human behavior. It is ignorant human behavior.

Educating children to take blind actions is irresponsible education, or no education at all. Most Western people will reply that it was through a set of firm behavior rules, so-called *morally correct behavior*, that positive karma could be created. However, *moral correctness* is on the same line as *political correctness*. It is a total fake as moral rules change from country to country and in some countries even from village to village, and they change over time as well, and they change fundamentally when economic conditions change.

Moralism is a fiction and one of the most sordid ways to blindfold the masses of ignorant citizens and keep them from educating themselves about the universal laws and rules that *really* regulate action and reaction.[42] How much morally correct behavior has triggered wars and genocide! How many massacres have been committed in the name of well-sounding moralistic slogans, how many millions of people killed for politically and morally correct principles! That the Western world, today, is caught in a cancerous and destructive death cycle is primarily the result of several millennia of moralistic tradition and education!

------

[42] http://ipublica.net/moralism/

The Myth of Normalcy

Normalcy does not exist in nature; it is a left–brain concept, a *pure intellectual construct*. The assumption that normalcy equals heterosexuality follows thus the same bias; heterosexuality as such is a concept, but nothing real. Sexuality is not a fixated condition; humans are not animals that unconsciously follow instinct and conditioning; human sexuality is not a drive – and here I am consciously contradicting Freud and sexology.

Human sexuality is not distinct, not abstract from human emotions; both emotions and sexuality are linked in that sex attraction follows emotional attraction, not *vice versa*. In addition human sexual attraction is not something that can be split off from the individual person; it is part of the soul level of the person and as such in itself invested with soul, with life, with vital energy. Not all in sexuality is teleological with the ultimate goal of (total) penetration; all is here subject to dialogue, to mutual bargain and discussion, to trial–and–error over time, to play–like fun, and so on. And the ultimate satisfaction is by the same token not always and I would even say typically not the sexual satisfaction as such but the *emotional satisfaction* or the congruence between emotional and sexual fulfillment with one and the same partner.[43]

This can well happen between an adult and a child, despite the obvious divergence in body size and genitals. I would even say that the very fact of the existence of *childlove* shows that nature has not programmed us like machines that

---

[43] http://emonics.net

do sex in a wheel–like manner or in a robotic obsession so that all fits in each other. I once said it in a poetic manner:

> – We are not machines, we are human beings. We are more like cigars, hand–made and individually differently shaded, some coming with broken leaves, some having a different tint. We are not like cigarettes, machine–produced, every single cigarette like any other one, exactly the same. There is no straight line in nature, only in human intellectualism.

Today's idea of sex is after all a sort of *compulsion to do sex*, which is a left–brain concept, a pure intellectual compulsion and it came up probably as an anti–reaction against patriarchal sex repression. It also is part of the competition culture where sex is most of the time a matter of *performance* which makes that many men are driven, time and again, into temporary, sporadic or even long–term impotence.

The Myth of Poverty

One does not need to know about *differential calculus* to see that we can never fight poverty as long as our national budgets allocate for military and defense purposes more than ten times the amount spent for education.

Instead of admitting the simple socioeconomic and political facts of life, most politicians try to veil this truth and instead come up with ideologies.

We had communism around long enough to see what it does with the human potential. And we have capitalism still around – for how long?

Neither the capitalist nor the communist model have found the way to sustain human potential and creative living in a non–destructive way. While the *capitalist model* blindfolds about the strangling effects of consumer credits, the *communist model* seems to totally disregard the human nature. This is why, I think, the capitalist model is still around, with all its inherent pitfalls of course, whereas the communist model has almost totally disappeared from the globe.

This being said, and positively put, it is well possible to end poverty by a deliberate global collaboration of responsible governments who, aided by private foundations and businesses, set out to really build a global community, a global market and a decent living for all peoples on the globe. It is well possible to reduce military expenses and it is well possible to dedicate a substantial share of our national budgets to the fight against poverty. But to get there, a will is needed – and this will is lacking. This is the reality and not what the media tell us as the mouth pieces of the status quo. The problem is that this will is lacking, both on the individual and the collective level. Those who are rich think that by sharing a part of their riches with those who have nothing, they will have less, they will be deprived, they will starve. *This is nonsense*. The contrary will be true.

If we can realize a truly global market, not a fake global market as we have it today, because in our global economy today less than twenty percent of the world population can participate, we will have much more, and in addition we'll have this much more with a much better conscience, with a much better feeling. The benefits cannot be seen in advance because growth is non–linear.

It cannot be grasped by linear, mathematical thought. In reality, once poverty is eliminated and all peoples on the globe able to participate in a truly global market, the *synergy* that is created through such a change *would be immense*, it would be so immense that no economics guru can ever adequately predict it.

And not only would we be so much richer, but our general life quality would be much higher because of the *positive vibrations* that this would create.

This is so because when human suffering is effectively reduced, positive and growth–fostering vibrations would virtually transform our lives and our environment. And war would be eliminated as well because war is well also a function of poverty, material poverty and poverty of comprehension typically going hand in hand.

Thus, whatever you think about poverty, you should at least be honest and when others come up with the same lies that are spread out in the media every day more, you should stand up and say :

> – No. I do not want to share. That's all. Period.

Then, at least you would be consistent.

The Myths of Religion

We are today facing a terrible violent mess called spirituality, in the West and in the East. What is the most obvious in this chaotic situation is the dishonesty that sells as spiritual or religious what is but a matter of confusion and false beliefs, or else a cunning poker of socioeconomic interests played out in the name of fundamentalism. We have to face it, without moving, and then only, if we can stand it without falling in the next horror trip, into the next depression or the next alcoholic or mescaline trip – we can make an evolution. That is how it is.

We are progressing despite all. You get the picture intellectually, but that is not it. The only solution is the heart, not the mind. Your knowledge from books does generally not help you much. What helps you is to gain awareness about yourself. But this quest to be yourself is impossible if you bury your feelings under a masquerade of –

- ▸ How should I be?

- ▸ How should I behave?

- ▸ How am I being adequate?

- ▸ How should I plan my future?

- ▸ How am I to grow?

- ▸ How am I to develop my full potential?

- ▸ How is life and what is it for me?

- What is the sense of all living?

- What is the sense of love?

- Why do we have sexual urges?

It's only after stopping to ask and accept life as it is and yourself as you are, and your being imperfect as a good and normal condition, that you can do any kind of evolution, and advance.

The Myth of Science

Any valid science is focused upon dealing with the dynamic patterns of living, and not with what these patterns have brought about. From this holistic perspective, our modern Western science is neither a science nor is it modern. By contrast, the *I Ching* that is five thousand years old, is both a true science and modern. It is a true scientific tool because it deals with the dynamic patterns of life and helps to identify them. And it is modern because its wisdom is without age, and still today fresh and new.[44]

With modern science it's as with modern medicine. It deals with the symptoms and not the cause of a disease. It looks at secondary effects instead of regarding the primary causes. Instead of understanding that life is coded in dynamic patterns, it has assumed that life was founded upon certain principles. What is the difference between patterns and principles?

---

[44] See also Pierre F. Walter, *Eight Dynamic Patterns of Living: Base Elements of True Civilization*, Audiobook (2010) and Essay (2012).

A pattern is a set of things, a certain *systemic arrangement* I can make out in the complex scheme of reality. It is something I can observe. A pattern can be fix or it can be changeable. It can be *static* or *dynamic*. By contrast, a *principle* typically is the beginning of a down–hierarchy, a top–something in a kind of up–to–down order. It is not something I can directly observe. It's but the outcome of a conclusion I draw intellectually after observing nature. A principle thus contains my observer point or my judgment about reality.

Death science looks at life through the glasses of principles it has set *before* it was going to observe. It is *essentially blind*, and it proceeds by imposing characteristics upon nature. Western science is death science. Traditionally, it has gained its first conclusions about life by vivisecting cadavers, not by observing the moving changes of living. It is, and remains, a cadaver science that is far removed from the changing patterns of reality.

Life science looks at life without any prefixed principles or assumptions and observes the dynamic patterns or changes in the texture of life. It is a science that since its start, around five thousand years ago, was interested in life, and draw conclusions from life, and not from death. Traditional Eastern science is life science, one branch of this very large body of science and philosophy being *Feng Shui*.[45] The *I Ching* is based upon life science, and is perhaps the highest condensation of it. Needless to add that, as such, it is non–judgmental and thus bears no moralistic judgments about human behavior. It

---

[45] http://ipublica.net/feng-shui/

looks at human behavior in exactly the same way it looks at all life patterns, and sees the changing nature of it before all.

Western scientific thought and traditional philosophy, ignorant about the fundamentals of the truth of the *bioenergy* as the primary creator force in the universe, was of course taking as real what it saw. As it saw matter only, it deducted that matter was the ultimate creator force, hence it assumed and formulated a basically materialistic scientific paradigm. However, this statement is valid only for mainstream science. As I have shown in various publications, even in times of the most fundamental repression of holistic pro–life wisdom in Europe, the original holistic life–science was taught and practiced in the underground by many alchemists and natural healers such as Paracelsus, to name only the most famous among them.[46]

Today, mainstream science is like a lazy school–boy, timidly learning lessons in dim afternoon classes it should have learnt, long ago, in the bright morning hours.

---

[46] See Pierre F. Walter, *Do You Love Einstein?*, Monograph (2010).

CREATING REALITY

Move on and leave your past behind you!, said the wizard, and you answer *Yes, this is all right and good, and I can see it with my rational mind, but the rest of myself does not seem to follow that insight. So I remain caught in the net woven by my past and my deeply ingrained habitual thought and emotional patterns.*

I have the habit to make myself down, says one. *I have the habit to make myself up*, says the other. They talk to each other and conclude they were *opposite characters*. In reality, they are very similar. Both make themselves down. The second one however has a narcissistic pattern in addition to his guilt–and–shame pattern which means that he covers his wound by counterfeiting his own knowledge, saying *I'm Peter Pan, and as such far removed from your petty world. I fly in the airs, catch me if you can.* The sane mind does not make itself down, nor up. It accepts itself and all–that–is. His reality is either perceived directly and without distortion, which is possible and to be found with spiritual coaches and shamans, or processed to a minimum extent because of a highly developed consciousness surface, which is a state of spiritual evolution each of us can attain.

The present second part of this essay is a short guide to assist you in this very important quest for self–development. We have seen in the first part of this production that most people are on the passive side of life, so to say, perceiving reality more or less unconsciously and processing that information as good as they can. Perhaps it is true what David Mahoney who was named in *Fortune Magazine* one of the ten toughest bosses in America, has to say about this subject:

David Mahoney

I just keep moving every day as hard and fast as I can. High–intensity and high–voltage. Light comes from that, not from passivity. I insist we all do our best every day. I'm intense in everything I do and I expect others will be, too. There may be timing factors in it, good luck and fortune factors, but the question is, do you utilize it? Some of it you can't control – some of it goes against you – it works both ways. You run to daylight – where you see the break you go. Most people aren't even aware of what's happening around them. Two–thirds of the people don't know what's going on to them, personally.[47]

I find it always amazing to see in which precise ways the insights of spiritual teachers, successful psychiatrists, famous artists and outstanding entrepreneurs coincide when it goes to explain the why and how of success. This tells me that this

---

[47] See Edward de Bono, *Tactics (1993)*.

information and insight is available to all of us, and not only to some chosen elite. *This insight is intuition.* What most mediocre people do is to foreclose, in one or the other way, this natural knowledge about high achievement in order to justify their limitative worldview and to have a reason for engaging in self-pity and endless procrastination.

In all great success there is an element of *novelty*, something that was hardly predictable before the person succeeded on their particular path. This element of novelty is what makes the essential part of success in that it is part of a new reality that has been created, consciously or implicitly. As Edward de Bono states it:

> – Once a new idea springs into existence it cannot be unthought.

No, I'm not talking about science fiction here. It's true that science fiction authors have been particularly imaginative for envisioning a *new global reality*, a new reality for the whole of humanity, and this particularly on a technological level. Here I'm talking about *personal reality*, not about the reality of a future humanity. I am not a science fiction author, nor a social utopist.

What I show you is not something related to myself, but something that is within *your own personal potential*. I show you an ability that you already possess, alongside your other skills and capacities. However, most people ignore that human *imagination* could have such a strong impact upon reality, and that it's actually a creator force, *the* creator force in the universe. Yet this tremendous energy has to be properly channeled. Your best imagination is not of much use when your general thought patterns are overwhelmingly negative.

Look at the life story of the great French novelist Honoré de Balzac, who was one of the most imaginative authors in the literary history of humanity.[48] And yet his personal life was a series of tragedies, failures, disasters, scandals, open or hidden fights with others, animosities of the worst sort, and on the other hand unbridled debauchery, self indulgence and a lifestyle in which he exhibited very little self–discipline.

Suffices to read one page of this literary genius, the description of a person, the way the hero or heroine is clothed, walks, talks, thinks and we are put directly on–stage, facing that person in real life, so vivid are Balzac's descriptions, so brilliant and sharp was his imagination. But to what *purpose* was it used? It was certainly used to create great literature and art. It was hardly ever, or not at all used to create a new and different personal reality for the author *himself.*

This is an example for the fact that imagination alone does not bring the result, but that all depends on how imagination is channeled. How do you *use* your imagination? And with which purpose do you use it, *when* you use it?

When your memory surface is not clear, what happens when you use imagination for achieving your goals? I cannot tell you what happens, but I can tell you that chances are low for what you wish to happen really to come about. Why? Because your memory surface intermittently infiltrates information in your imaginative content that you absolutely do not

---

[48] http://ipublica.net/honore-de-balzac/

wish to have put. Is there any willful control over this process? No. There is only one way: *clearing* the memory surface. When your glasses are dirty, and you see a foggy world, your willpower alone will not clean them. You have to take a piece of cloth and wipe them clean. It's the same with memory. It can be wiped clean.

I have done that at several instances in my life and thus I know that it works. You may have read in other books that it does not work, or that it works only for very exceptional people such as yogis, gurus, spiritual teachers, and the like.

No, we are talking here about *something ordinary*, not about a mysterious spiritual matter. We are talking about something rather mechanical. The memory surface pretty much works like a magnetic tape. It can store information. It can add–on information. It can erase information. Only one thing it cannot do. There is no function that stops the brain from recording.

This means that even though you may already program your reality according to your innermost wishes, reality always brings novelty of its own, because it's not, and cannot be, dependent upon your creative mind. That's a truth that our great poets express beautifully and that can be put very simply in the formula: reality always surpasses the individual mind. But that's not something to deplore. It only shows that our individual mind and soul are *imbedded* in a greater soul reality that kind of connects all minds within a cosmic meta–reality that is beyond the control of our individual mind. And yet, every impact of our individual mind upon this cosmic reality surface is noticed and can be retraced.

I have explained this in order to prevent you from getting depressed by just another pitfall of perception, this time of self–perception: the pitfall namely to believe we were *insignificant* as individual human beings on that cosmic, universal plane of consciousness. If this was so, we could not be co–creators, and we could not create our own reality. And in that case, I would not have taken the time and done the effort to tell you all of this.

A philosopher once compared humans with the billions of grains of sand on a beach, and this image has been interpreted as a metaphor for the insignificance of human beings in the cosmos. This is, in my view, a fundamental error.

Who, tell me, *knows* about the importance of an individual grain of sand in the whole of the cosmos, or even the whole of creation? To arrogate yourself to state that a grain of sand is insignificant means the same as saying that the whole of creation, and implicitly also that the creator force itself is insignificant. Today we know through *quantum physics* that every single electron, every single particle, that is only a tiny, very tiny fraction of a grain of sand, is conscious, and maintains relationships, chooses partners and friends, and locations, or remains undecided and at many locations at the same time.

Particles are *conscious*. And if that is true, by implication, grains of sand are conscious. And thus they are *alive!*

There are various methods to clear the memory surface. In order to make a good choice, you need to know more details about what memory actually is. Forget what you heard in school about it as it's most probably wrong. Memory is not in the brain, but in the *luminous body* or *aura*. It's coded in energy patterns and these patterns are virtually flowing around you, they are in movement, not static. The brain acts as interface to the memory surface; it does *not* store information. The old scientific view of the brain as a storage house is long superseded by newest research that, eventually, has included the insights we gain from parapsychology, clairvoyant research, Chinese medicine and acupuncture, and meditation, as well as quantum physics.[49]

To conclude from this research, we can say that memory is volatile; this has, by the way, a big advantage, namely, that memory is *not forever engraved anywhere in our gray matter*, as it was believed by a mechanistic neurology of the 1960s and 70s. It also means that memory can be triggered to release information by touching parts of the body, by doing certain movements, by doing body work such as *Rolfing* or *Alexander Technique*.

Reichian massage has proven to be especially conducive to releasing old memory patterns from the orgone shell or aura that permeates our organism, both inside the cell and around our physical body. I have also analyzed more recent techniques like Dr. Villoldo's *soul retrieval* and reviewed some of his books.[50] There is more information in my *Idiot Guide to Emotions (2010)*.

---

[49] Shafica Karagulla, *The Chakras (1989)*, Charles W. Leadbeater, *The Inner Life (1911)*. See also Pierre F. Walter, *Alternative Medicine and Wellness Techniques*, Scholarly Article (2011).

[50] Alberto Villoldo, *Mending the Past and Healing the Future With Soul Retrieval (2005)*.

The second important point to know about memory is that it's not memory itself that creates hangups, addictions, habits or obsessions we may suffer from, but the *emotional entanglement* with past events and hurts that is a typical side–effect of trauma and abuse. It is entanglement that makes us repeat again and again the same scenarios in life, as our inner intelligence puts them on stage for us to get out of the strings, and heal our past.

The vicious circle in this is that when people are unconscious and blame life, god or others for their misfortunes, they are blocking the potential healing of their scars. Then they remain entangled, and perhaps so for their whole lifetime. That is why *emonic consciousness* is so important; it is *energy consciousness*, an awareness of the flow of energy in our organism, which includes awareness of *where and how our energy flow is blocked* or obstructed in certain parts of the body. Typically, it's the parts of the body that have been concerned when the abuse or traumatic event happened.

Now, how to build emonic or emotional awareness? The paradox that I found is that there is no technique to bring that awareness about when using our rational mind; it has to be built unconsciously, by sharpening our intuition.

How, then? The old Chinese saying *Nonaction is action* says it all in a way, when it's understood what this saying means. My experience with healing has taught me that it means to *not directly interfere* in the process, as this may strengthen the evil, so to speak. Let me give you one example for this from the book *Getting Well Again (1978/1992)* by the physician Dr.

Carl Simonton.[51] Dr. Simonton, who runs one of the most successful alternative therapies for cancer in California, reports in his book that many cancer patients who go to energy healers or laying–on of hands practitioners experience their cancer to grow, and not to shrink, after the treatment.[52]

Why? Dr. Simonton says that cancer cells are very eager to receive energy, which lets them grow even more. This is an example that shows that a direct interference in the disease pattern does often not bring relief. And by the way, an operation, for example the removal of a cancerous tumor, is just another of these direct interventions; and it has been reported, by Simonton, and others, that removing a cancerous tumor does not per se remove the cancer, as the cancer is not in the tumor.

The tumor is only a *secondary effect*, one of many, of the cancer. This is why many cancer patients have made the sad experience that after having suffered a severe removal or amputation of an organ or limb, the cancer was beginning to spread elsewhere in the body.

So let me take this as a metaphor for introducing the simple yet effective technique I came to use for coping with hurtful memories; and let me add also that the expression *erasing the memory surface* is of course a metaphor as well. The process is much more complex in reality.

The technique I found helpful and effective for healing early trauma is *creative writing*. I came to realize it during a

---

[51] Dr. O. Carl Simonton, et al.: *Getting Well Again (1978/1992)*.

[52] http://www.simontoncenter.com/

hypnotherapy twenty years ago, when my psychiatrist gave me certain themes to write about, asking me certain precise questions about my parents. I carried out these assignments very seriously and meticulously, and made the amazing discovery, that later was confirmed by my psychiatrist, that the actual healing took place every time *before* I had the next session with my psychiatrist, and thus actually before I presented those memoirs to him. He would utter something like we would not need to do any work, and can just 'chat a little today', as the big change was obvious and could even be seen in my face.

This dumbfounded me at first, but I had to report that indeed every time I wrote one of those little stories, a great calm came over me, an inner peace I had not known before, and I felt very clearly the stream of hot vital energy flowing through my whole organism, while before I felt the energy was stuck in my lower legs and my pelvis region, which is why I had icy feet most of the time. That problem with icy feet that I had been suffering from since my late adolescence was completely solved after writing the stories, and did no more recur later on in life.

On the other hand I have to say that honestly the writing itself was most of the time not a very agreeable experience.

The jotting down of those hurtful events, or in case the memory was only scarcely intact, the whole scenery or *taste* of a certain period of my life, triggered rather unwelcome body reactions, like outbursts of heat, hot rage, strong sweating, or sexual arousal, or *all of this at once* in a frenzy Draculian bath of violence that I can only compare with the eruption of a vulcan. At other times the body seemed to *shrink and mourn*, and I felt like a small fly in a universe of ice, where there are endless pathways in the dark, and icy chambers with rotten souls everywhere. Then I would fall in a deep depression and had suicidal ideas.

Both the violent reactions and the suicidal ones were even stronger when I did not only the writing, but also used spontaneous art for triggering the inner healing. That is why I suggest to beginners to *not do both at the same time*, at least not when you are alone and have no psychiatric support at your side.[53]

If you are serious about creating your own reality, instead of consuming the infected reality of the bulk of unconscious road–runners that populate this globe for too long, you also have to start with *Life Authoring*.[54] You may also want to begin practicing a body consciousness technique such as Tai Chi Chuan.[55] Last not least the excellent movie *What the Bleep Do We Know, Quantum Edition* offers many viable suggestions and scientific corroboration of the possibility to create our own personal reality – for good![56] And when you look over the fence, and in the art world, you may realize that some

---

[53] See, more in detail, Pierre F. Walter, *Child Play: Coaching Your Inner Child*, Audiobook (2010), Essay (2012).

[54] http://authoryourlife.com
http://ipublica.com/author-your-life/
http://ipublica.net/life-authoring/

[55] Master Liang, Shou–Yu, *Simplified Tai Chi Chuan (1996)*.

[56] http://ipublica.net/what-the-bleep-do-we-know/

artists have done extremely well in creating new art reality.
Let me mention only *Pablo Picasso* and *Svjatoslav Richter* here as
examples while there are of course many more, but I know
these particularly well.[57]

These great artists provide excellent examples for *reality
creation*; they have not only revolutionized their specific
branch of artistry, painting, and musical performance, re-
spectively, but with their strong personalities they have
coined, each, a grandiose universe.

Let me close this chapter with two quotes from the book
The Power of Your Subconscious Mind by Dr. Joseph Murphy:

Joseph Murphy

> Look around you. Wherever you live, whatever
> circle of society you are part of, you will notice
> that the vast majority of people lives in the world
> without. Those who are more enlightened, how-
> ever, are intensely involved with the world within.
> They realize – as you will, too – that the world
> within *creates* the world without. Your thoughts,
> feelings, and visualized imagery are the organiz-
> ing principles of your experience. The world
> within is the only creative power. Everything you
> find in your world of expression has been created
> by you in the inner world of your mind, whether
> consciously or unconsciously.[58]
>
> You must ask believing, if you are to receive.
> Your mind moves from the thought to the thing.
> Unless there is first an image in the mind, it can-
> not move, for there would be nothing for it to

---

[57] http://ipublica.net/pablo-picasso/
http://svjatoslavrichter.com

[58] Joseph Murphy, *The Power of Your Subconscious Mind (1963)*, p. 8.

move toward. Your prayer, which is your mental act, must be accepted as an image in your mind before the power from your subconscious will play upon it and make it productive. You must reach a point of acceptance in your mind, an unqualified and undisputed state of agreement.[59]

---

[59] Id., p. 79.

BIBLIOGRAPHY

Complete Bibliography

A

Abrams, Jeremiah (Ed.)

Reclaiming the Inner Child
New York: Tarcher/Putnam, 1990

Die Befreiung des Inneren Kindes
Die Wiederentdeckung unserer ursprünglichen kreativen Persönlichkeit
und ihre zentrale Bedeutung für unser Erwachsenwerden
München: Scherz Verlag, 1993

Adrienne, Carol

The Numerology Kit
New American Library, 1988

Agni Yoga Society

COEUR : Signes de l'Agni Yoga
Toulon: Sté Edipub, 1985
Publication originale date de 1932

Albrecht, Karl

The Only Thing That Matters
New York: Harper & Row, 1993

Alston, John P. / Tucker, Francis

The Myth of Sexual Permissiveness
The Journal of Sex Research, 9/1 (1973)

Appleton, Matthew

A Free Range Childhood
Self-Regulation at Summerhill School
Foundation for Educational Renewal, 2000

Summerhill
Kindern ihre Kindheit zurückgeben
Demokratie und Selbstregulierung in der Erziehung
Hohengehren: Schneider Verlag, 2003

Arcas, Gérald, Dr

Guérir le corps par l'hypnose et l'auto-hypnose
Paris: Sand, 1997

Ariès, Philippe

L'enfant et la famille sous l'Ancien Régime
Paris, Seuil, 1975

Centuries of Childhood
New York: Vintage Books, 1962

Geschichte der Kindheit
Frankfurt/M: DTV, 1998

Arntz, William & Chasse, Betsy

What the Bleep Do We Know
20th Century Fox, 2005 (DVD)

Down The Rabbit Hole Quantum Edition
20th Century Fox, 2006 (3 DVD Set)

Bleep
An der Schnittstelle von Spiritualität und Wissenschaft
Verblüffende Erkenntnisse und Anstösse zum Weiterdenken
Berlin: Vak Verlag, 2007

Arroyo, Stephen

Astrology, Karma & Transformation
The Inner Dimensions of the Birth Chart
Sebastopol, CA: CRSC Publications, 1978

Astrologie, Karma und Transformation
Die Chancen schwieriger Aspekte
Frankfurt/M: Heyne Verlag, 1998

Relationships and Life Cycles
Astrological Patterns of Personal Experience
Sebastopol, CA: CRCS Publications, 1993

Handbuch der Horoskop-Deutung
Berlin: Rowohlt, 1999

Atlee, Tom

The Tao of Democracy
Using Co-Intelligence to Create a World That Works for All
North Charleston, SC: Imprint Books / WorldWorks Press, 2003

B

Bachelard, Gaston

The Poetics of Reverie
Translated by Daniel Russell
Boston: Beacon Press, 1971

Poetik des Raumes
Frankfurt/M: Fischer Verlag, 2001

Bachofen, Johann Jakob

Gesammelte Werke, Band II
Das Mutterrecht
Basel: Benno Schwabe & Co., 1948
Erstveröffentlichung im Jahre 1861

Baggins, David Sadofsky

Drug Hate and the Corruption of American Justice
Santa Barbara: Praeger, 1998

Bagley, Christopher

Child Abusers
Research and Treatment
New York: Universal Publishers, 2003

Balter, Michael

The Goddess and the Bull
Catalhoyuk, An Archaeological Journey
to the Dawn of Civilization
New York: Free Press, 2006

Bandler, Richard

Get the Life You Want
The Secrets to Quick and Lasting Life Change
With Neuro-Linguistic Programming
Deerfield Beach, Fl: HCI, 2008

Barbaree, Howard E. & Marshall, William L. (Eds.)

The Juvenile Sex Offender
Second Edition
New York: Guilford Press, 2008

Barnes, A. James, Dworkin, Terry and Richards Eric L.

Law for Business, 9th Edition
New York: McGraw-Hill, 2006

Barnes, J. (Ed.)

The Complete Works of Aristotle, Vol. 1
Princeton: Princeton University Press, 1971

Barron, Frank X., Montuori, et al. (Eds.)

Creators on Creating
Awakening and Cultivating the Imaginative Mind
(New Consciousness Reader)
New York: P. Tarcher/Putnam, 1997

Bateson, Gregory

Steps to an Ecology of Mind
Chicago: University of Chicago Press, 2000
Originally published in 1972

Bender Lauretta & Blau, Abram

The Reaction of Children to Sexual Relations with Adults
American J. Orthopsychiatry 7 (1937), 500-518

Benkler, Yochai

The Wealth of Networks
How Social Production Transforms Markets and Freedom
New Haven, CT: Yale University Press, 2007

Bennion, Francis

Statutory Interpretation
London: Butterworths, 1984

Bernard, Frits

Paedophilia
A Factual Report
Amsterdam: Enclave, 1985

Pädophilie ohne Grenzen
Theorie, Forschung, Praxis
Frankfurt/M: Foerster Verlag, 1997

Kinderschänder?
Pädophilie, von der Liebe mit Kindern
3. Auflage
Frankfurt/M: Foerster Verlag, 1982

Bertalanffy, Ludwig von

General Systems Theory
Foundations, Development, Applications
New York: George Brazilier Publishing, 1976

Besant, Annie

An Autobiography
New Delhi: Penguin Books, 2005
Originally published in 1893

Karma
4e édition
Paris: Adyar, 1923

Bettelheim, Bruno

A Good Enough Parent
New York: A. Knopf, 1987

The Uses of Enchantment
New York: Vintage Books, 1989

Kinder brauchen Märchen
Frankfurt/M: DTV, 2002

Beutler/Bieber/Pipkorn/Streil

Die Europäische Gemeinschaft
Rechtsordnung und Politik
2. Auflage
Baden-Baden: Nomos, 1982

Block, Peter

Stewardship
Choosing Service Over Self-Interest
San Francisco: Berrett-Koehler, 1996

Blofeld, J.

The Book of Changes
A New Translation of the Ancient Chinese I Ching
New York: E.P. Dutton, 1965

Blum, Ralph H. & Laughan, Susan

The Healing Runes
Tools for the Recovery of Body, Mind, Heart & Soul
New York: St. Martin's Press, 1995

Boadalla, David

Wilhelm Reich, Leben und Werk
Frankfurt/M: Fischer, 1980

Bodin, Jean

On Sovereignty (1576)
Six Books of the Commonwealth
Edited by Professor Julian Franklin
New York: Seven Treasures Publications, 2009

Böhm, Wilfried

Maria Montessori
2. Auflage
Bad Heilbrunn: Julius Klinkhardt, 1991

Bohm, David

Wholeness and the Implicate Order
London: Routledge, 2002

Die implizite Ordnung
Grundlagen eines dynamischen Holismus
München: Goldmann Wilhelm, 1989

Thought as a System
London: Routledge, 1994

Quantum Theory
London: Dover Publications, 1989

La plénitude de l'univers
Paris: Rocher, 1992

La conscience de l'univers
Paris: Rocher, 1992

Boldt, Laurence G.

Zen and the Art of Making a Living
A Practical Guide to Creative Career Design
New York: Penguin Arkana, 1993

How to Find the Work You Love
New York: Penguin Arkana, 1996

Zen Soup
Tasty Morsels of Zen Wisdom From Great Minds East & West
New York: Penguin Arkana, 1997

The Tao of Abundance
Eight Ancient Principles For Abundant Living
New York: Penguin Arkana, 1999

Das Tao der Fülle
Vom Reichtum, der uns glücklich macht
Mittelberg: Joy Verlag, 2001

Bordeaux-Szekely, Edmond

Teaching of the Essenes from Enoch to the Dead
Sea Scrolls
Beekman Publishing, 1992

Gospel of the Essenes
The Unknown Books of the Essenes
& Lost Scrolls of the Essene Brotherhood
Beekman Publishing, 1988

Gospel of Peace of Jesus Christ
Beekman Publishing, 1994

Gospel of Peace, 2d Vol.
I B S International Publishers

Das Friedensevangelium der Essener
Saarbrücken: Neue Erde/Lentz, 2002

Évangile essénien de la paix
La vie biogénique
Genève: Éditions Soleil, 1978

Die unbekannten Schriften der Essener
Saarbrücken: Neue Erde/Lentz, 2002

Branden, Nathaniel

How to Raise Your Self-Esteem
New York: Bantam, 1987

Die 6 Säulen des Selbstwertgefühls
Erfolgreich und zufrieden durch ein starkes Selbst
München: Piper Verlag, 2009

Brant & Tisza

The Sexually Misused Child
American J. Orthopsychiatry, 47(1)(1977)

Brassai

Conversations with Picasso
Chicago: University of Chicago Publications, 1999

Brennan, Barbara Ann

Hands of Healing
A Guide to Healing Through the Human Energy Field
New York: Bantam, 1988

Brongersma, Edward

Aggression against Pedophiles
7 International Journal of Law & Psychiatry 82 (1984)

Loving Boys
Amsterdam, New York: GAP, 1987

Das verfemte Geschlecht
Berlin: Lichtenberg Verlag, 1970

Bruce, Alexandra

Beyond the Bleep
The Definite Unauthorized Guide to 'What the Bleep Do we Know!?'
New York: Disinformation, 2005

Bullough & Bullough (Eds.)

Human Sexuality
An Encyclopedia
New York: Garland Publishing, 1994

Sin, Sickness and Sanity
A History of Sexual Attitudes
New York: New American Library, 1977

Burgess, Ann Wolbert

Child Pornography and Sex Rings
New York: Lexington Books, 1984

Burwick, Frederick

The Damnation of Newton
Goethe's Color Theory and Romantic Perception
New York: Walter de Gruyter, 1986

Butler-Bowden, Tom

50 Success Classics
Winning Wisdom for Work & Life From 50 Landmark Books
London: Nicholas Brealey Publishing, 2004

50 Klassiker des Erfolgs
Die wichtigsten Werke von Kenneth Blanchard, Warren Buffet,
Andrew Carnegie, Stephen R. Covey, Spencer Johnson,
Benjamin Franklin, Napoleon Hill, Nelson Mandela, Anthony Robbins,
Brian Tracy, Sun Tsu, Jack Welch und vielen anderen
Frankfurt/M: MVG Verlag, 2005

50 Lebenshilfe Klassiker
Frankfurt/M: MVG Verlag, 2004

50 Klassiker der Psychologie
Die wichtigsten Werke von Alfred Adler, Sigmund Freud,
Daniel Goleman, Karen Horney, William James, C.G. Jung, Jean Piaget,
Viktor Frankl, Howard Gardner, Alfred Kinsey, Abraham Maslow, Iwan
Pawlow, Stanley Milgram, Martin Seligman und vielen anderen
Frankfurt/M: MVG Verlag, 2004

50 Klassiker der Spiritualität
Die wichtigsten Werke von Augustinus, Khalil Gibran, Mahatma Ghandi,
Dag Hammarskjölkd, Hermann Hesse, C. G. Jung, Eckhart Tolle,
J. Krishnamurti, Thich Nhat Hanh, Mutter Teresa, Dan Millman
und vielen anderen
Frankfurt/M: MVG Verlag, 2006

Buxton, Richard
The Complete World of Greek Mythology
London: Thames & Hudson, 2007

C

Cain, Chelsea & Moon Unit Zappa
Wild Child
New York: Seal Press (Feminist Publishing), 1999

Calderone & Ramey
Talking With Your Child About Sex
New York: Random House, 1982

Campbell, Herbert James

The Pleasure Areas
London: Eyre Methuen Ltd., 1973

Der Irrtum mit der Seele
München: Scherz Verlag, 1973

Les principes du plaisir
Paris: Stock, 1974

Campbell, Jacqueline C.

Assessing Dangerousness
Violence by Sexual Offenders, Batterers and Child
Abusers
New York: Sage Publications, 2004

Campbell, Joseph

The Hero With A Thousand Faces
Princeton: Princeton University Press, 1973
(Bollingen Series XVII)
London: Orion Books, 1999

Der Heros in Tausend Gestalten
München: Insel Verlag, 2009

Occidental Mythology
Princeton: Princeton University Press, 1973
(Bollingen Series XVII)
New York: Penguin Arkana, 1991

The Masks of God
Oriental Mythology
New York: Penguin Arkana, 1992
Originally published 1962

Mythologie des Ostens
Die Masken Gottes Bd. 2
Basel: Sphinx Verlag, 1996

The Power of Myth
With Bill Moyers
ed. by Sue Flowers
New York: Anchor Books, 1988

Die Kraft der Mythen
Düsseldorf: Patmos Verlag, 2007

Cantelon, Philip L. (Ed.)

The American Atom
A Documentary History of Nuclear Policies from the
Discovery of Fission to the Present
With Richard G. Hewlett (Ed.) and Robert C. Williams (Ed.)
Philadelphia, PA: University of Pennsylvania Press, 1992

Capacchione, Lucia

The Power of Your Other Hand
North Hollywood, CA: Newcastle Publishing, 1988

Capra, Bernt Amadeus

Mindwalk
A Film for Passionate Thinkers
Based Upon Fritjof Capra's *The Turning Point*
New York: Triton Pictures, 1990

Capra, Fritjof

The Turning Point
Science, Society And The Rising Culture
New York: Simon & Schuster, 1987
Original Author Copyright, 1982

Wendezeit
Bausteine für ein neues Weltbild
München: Droemer Knaur, 2004

Le temps du changement
Science, société et nouvelle culture
Paris: Rocher, 1994

The Tao of Physics
An Exploration of the Parallels Between Modern
Physics and Eastern Mysticism
New York: Shambhala Publications, 2000
(New Edition) Originally published in 1975

Das Tao der Physik
Die Konvergenz von westlicher Wissenschaft und östlicher Philosophie
Neue und erweiterte Auflage
München: O.W. Barth bei Scherz, 2000
Ursprünglich erschienen 1975 bei Droemersche Verlagsanstalt
in Hamburg

Le tao de la physique
Paris: Sand & Tchou, 1994

The Web of Life
A New Scientific Understanding of Living Systems
New York: Doubleday, 1997
Author Copyright 1996

Lebensnetz
Ein neues Verständnis der lebendigen Welt
München: Scherz Verlag, 1999

The Hidden Connections
Integrating The Biological, Cognitive And Social
Dimensions Of Life Into A Science Of Sustainability
New York: Doubleday, 2002

Verborgene Zusammenhänge
München: Scherz, 2002

Steering Business Toward Sustainability
New York: United Nations University Press, 1995

Uncommon Wisdom
Conversations with Remarkable People
New York: Bantam, 1989

The Science of Leonardo
Inside the Mind of the Great Genius of the Renaissance
New York: Anchor Books, 2008
New York: Bantam Doubleday, 2007 (First Publishing)

Complete List of Publications
http://www.fritjofcapra.net/publishers.html

Cassou, Michelle & Cubley, Steward

Life, Paint and Passion
Reclaiming the Magic of Spontaneous Expression
New York: P. Tarcher/Putnam, 1996

Castaneda, Carlos

The Teachings of Don Juan
A Yaqui Way of Knowledge
Washington: Square Press, 1985

Journey to Ixtlan
Washington: Square Press: 1991

Tales of Power
Washington: Square Press, 1991

The Second Ring of Power
Washington: Square Press, 1991

Castel, Robert

L'ordre psychiatrique, l'âge d'or de l'aliénisme
Paris: Éditions de Minuit, 1977

Cayce, Edgar

Modern Prophet
Four Complete Books
'Edgar Cayce On Prophecy'
'Edgar Cayce On Religion and Psychic Experience'
'Edgar Cayce On Mysteries of the Mind'

'Edgar Cayce On Reincarnation'
By Mary Ellen Carter
Ed. by Hugh Lynn Cayce
New York: Random House, 1968

Chaplin, Charles

My Autobiography
New York: Plume, 1992
Originally published in 196

Chevalier, Jean & Gheerbrant, Alain

A Dictionary of Symbols
Translated from the French by John Buchanan-Brown
New York: Penguin, 1996

Cho, Susanne

Kindheit und Sexualität im Wandel der Kulturgeschichte
Eine Studie zur Bedeutung der kindlichen Sexualität unter besonderer
Berücksichtigung des 17. und 20. Jahrhunderts
Zürich, 1983 (Doctoral thesis)

Chopra, Deepak

Creating Affluence
The A-to-Z Steps to a Richer Life
New York: Amber-Allen Publishing (2003)

Life After Death
The Book of Answers
London: Rider, 2006

Leben nach dem Tod
Das letzte Geheimnis unserer Existenz
Berlin: Allegria Verlag, 2008

Synchrodestiny
Discover the Power of Meaningful Coincidence to Manifest Abundance
Audio Book / CD
Niles, IL: Nightingale-Conant, 2006

The Seven Spiritual Laws of Success
A Practical Guide to the Fulfillment of Your Dreams
Audio Book / CD
New York: Amber-Allen Publishing (2002)

Die Sieben Geistigen Gesetze des Erfolgs
Berlin: Ullstein Verlag, 2004

The Spontaneous Fulfillment of Desire
Harnessing the Infinite Power of Coincidence
New York: Random House Audio, 2003

Cicero, Marcus Tullius

Selected Works
New York: Penguin, 1960 (Penguin Classics)

Clarke, Ronald

Einstein: The Life and Times
New York: Avon Books, 1970

Clarke-Steward, S., Friedman, S. & Koch, J.

Child Development, A Topical Approach
London: John Wiley, 1986

Cleary, Thomas

The Taoist I Ching
Translated by Thomas Cleary
Boston & London: Shambhala, 1986

Constantine, Larry L.

Children & Sex
New Findings, New Perspectives
Larry L. Constantine & Floyd M. Martinson (Eds.)
Boston: Little, Brown & Company, 1981

Treasures of the Island
Children in Alternative Lifestyles
Beverly Hills: Sage Publications, 1976

Where are the Kids?
in: Libby & Whitehurst (ed.)
Marriage and Alternatives
Glenview: Scott Foresman, 1977

Open Family
A Lifestyle for Kids and other People
26 FAMILY COORDINATOR 113-130 (1977)

Cook, M. & Howells, K. (Eds.)
Adult Sexual Interest in Children
Academic Press, London, 1980

Coudenhove-Kalergi, Richard N.
Paneuropa
Wien-Leipzig: Paneuropa Verlag, 1926

Covey, Stephen R.
The 7 Habits of Highly Effective People
Powerful Lessons in Personal Change
New York: Free Press, 2004
15th Anniversary Edition
First Published in 1989

Die 7 Wege zur Effektivität
Prinzipien für persönlichen und beruflichen Erfolg
Offenbach: Gabal Verlag, 2009

The 8th Habit
From Effectiveness to Greatness
London: Simon & Schuster, 2004

Der 8. Weg
Von der Effektivität zur wahren Grösse
Offenbach: Gabal Verlag, 2006

Covitz, Joel

Emotional Child Abuse
The Family Curse
Boston: Sigo Press, 1986

Cox, Geraldine

The Home is Where the Heart is
Sydney: Macmillan, 2000

Craze, Richard

Feng Shui
Feng Shui Book & Card Pack
London: Thorsons, 1997

Cross, Sir Rupert

Cross on Evidence
5th ed.
London: Butterworths, 1979

Introduction to Criminal Law
10th Edition
London: Butterworths, 1984

Currier, Richard L.

Juvenile Sexuality in Global Perspective
in : Children & Sex, New Findings, New Perspectives
Larry L. Constantine & Floyd M. Martinson (Eds.)
Boston: Little, Brown & Company, 1981

D

Daco, Pierre

Les triomphes de la psychanalyse de Pierre Daco
Bruxelles: Éditions Gérard & Co., 1965 (Marabout)

Dalai Lama

Ethics for the New Millennium
New York: Penguin Putnam, 1999

David-Neel, Alexandra

Magic and Mystery in Tibet
New York: Dover Publications, 1971

The Secret Oral Teachings in Tibetan Buddhist Sects
New York: Secrets of Light Publishers, 1981

Initiations and Initiates in Tibet
New York: Dover Publications, 1993

Immortality and Reincarnation
Wisdom from the Forbidden Journey
New York: Inner Tradition, 1997

Davidson, Gustav

A Dictionary of Angels
Including Fallen Angels
New York: Free Press, 1967

Davis, A. J.

Sexual Assaults in the Philadelphia Prison System and Sheriff's Van
Trans-Action 6, 2, 8-16 (1968)

Dean & Bruyn-Kops

The Crime and the Consequences of Rape
New York: Thomas, 1982

De Bono, Edward

The Use of Lateral Thinking
New York: Penguin, 1967

The Mechanism of Mind
New York: Penguin, 1969

Sur/Petition
London: HarperCollins, 1993

Tactics
London: HarperCollins, 1993
First published in 1985

Taktiken und Strategien erfolgreicher Menschen
Frankfurt/M: MVG Verlag, 1995

Serious Creativity
Using the Power of Lateral Thinking to Create New Ideas
London: HarperCollins, 1996

Delacour, Jean-Baptiste

Glimpses of the Beyond
New York: Bantam Dell, 1975

Deleuze, Gilles, Guattari, Felix

L'Anti-Oedipe
Capitalisme et Schizophrénie
Nouvelle Édition Augmentée
Paris: Éditions de Minuit, 1973

DeMause, Lloyd

The History of Childhood
New York, 1974

Foundations of Psychohistory
New York: Creative Roots, 1982

DeMeo, James

Heretic's Notebook
Emotions, Protocells, Ether-Drift and Cosmic Life Energy
with New Research Supporting Wilhelm Reich
Pulse of the Planet, #5 (2002)
Ashland, Oregon: Orgone Biophysical Research Laboratories, Inc., 2002

Nach Reich, Neue Forschungen zur Orgonomie
Sexualökonomie / Die Entdeckung der Orgonenergie
Herausgegeben zusammen mit Professor Bernd Senf, Berlin
Frankfurt/M: Zweitausendeins Verlag, 1997

Saharasia
The 4000 BCE Origins of Child Abuse, Sex-Repression,
Warfare and Social Violence in the Deserts of the Old World
Ashland, Oregon: Orgone Biophysical Research Laboratories, Inc., 1998

Deshimaru, Taisen

Zen et vie quotidienne
Paris: Albin Michel, 1985

Diamond, Stephen A., May, Rollo

Anger, Madness, and the Daimonic
The Psychological Genesis of Violence, Evil and Creativity
New York: State University of New York Press, 1999

DiCarlo, Russell E. (Ed.)

Towards A New World View
Conversations at the Leading Edge
Erie, PA: Epic Publishing, 1996

Dicta et Françoise

Tarot de Marseille
Paris: Mercure de France, 1980

Dolto, Françoise

La Cause des Enfants
Paris: Laffont, 1985

Mein Leben auf der Seite der Kinder
Ein Plädoyer für eine kindgerechte Welt
Hamburg: Lübbe Verlagsgruppe, 1993

Psychanalyse et Pédiatrie
Paris: Seuil, 1971

Psychoanalyse und Kinderheilkunde
Frankfurt/M: Suhrkamp, 1997

Séminaire de Psychanalyse d'Enfants, 1
Paris: Seuil, 1982

Séminaire de Psychanalyse d'Enfants, 2
Paris: Seuil, 1985

Séminaire de Psychanalyse d'Enfants, 3
Paris: Seuil, 1988

Praxis der Kinderanalyse. Ein Seminar.
Hamburg: Klett-Cotta, 1985

Alles ist Sprache
Kindern mit Worten helfen
Berlin: Quadriga, 1996

Über das Begehren
Die Anfänge der menschlichen Kommunikation
2. Auflage
Hamburg: Klett-Cotta, 1996

Kinder stark machen
Die ersten Lebensjahre
Berlin: Beltz Verlag, 2000

L'évangile au risque de la psychanalyse
Paris: Seuil, 1980

Dover, K.J.
Greek Homosexuality
New York: Fine Communications, 1997

Dreher & Tröndle

Strafgesetzbuch und Nebengesetze
42. Aufl.
München: Beck, 1985

Dürckheim, Karlfried Graf

Hara: The Vital Center of Man
Rochester: Inner Traditions, 2004

Hara
Die Erdmitte des Menschen
Neuausgabe
München: O.W. Barth bei Scherz, 2005

Zen and Us
New York: Penguin Arkana 1991

The Call for the Master
New York: Penguin Books, 1993

Absolute Living
The Otherworldly in the World and the Path to Maturity
New York: Penguin Arkana, 1992

The Way of Transformation
Daily Life as a Spiritual Exercise
London: Allen & Unwin, 1988

Der Alltag als Übung
Vom Weg der Verwandlung
Bern: Huber, 2008

The Japanese Cult of Tranquility
London: Rider, 1960

Kultur der Stille
Frankfurt/M: Weltz Verlag, 1997

E

Eden, Donna & Feinstein, David

Energy Medicine
New York: Tarcher/Putnam, 1998

The Energy Medicine Kit
Simple Effective Techniques to Help You Boost Your Vitality
Boulder, Co.: Sounds True Editions, 2004

The Promise of Energy Psychology
With David Feinstein and Gary Craig
Revolutionary Tools for Dramatic Personal Change
New York: Jeremy P. Tarcher/Penguin, 2005

Edmunds, Francis

An Introduction to Anthroposophy
Rudolf Steiner's Worldview
London: Rudolf Steiner Press, 2005

Edwardes, A.

The Jewel of the Lotus
New York, 1959

Einstein, Albert

The World As I See It
New York: Citadel Press, 1993

Mein Weltbild
Berlin: Ullstein, 2005

Out of My Later Years
New York: Outlet, 1993

Ideas and Opinions
New York: Bonanza Books, 1988

Einstein sagt
Zitate, Einfälle, Gedanken
München: Piper, 2007

Albert Einstein Notebook
London: Dover Publications, 1989

Eisler, Riane

The Chalice and the Blade
Our history, Our future
San Francisco: Harper & Row, 1995

Kelch und Schwert, Unsere Geschichte, unsere Zukunft
Weibliches und männliches Prinzip in der Geschichte
Freiburg: Arbor Verlag, 2005

Sacred Pleasure: Sex, Myth and the Politics of the Body
New Paths to Power and Love
San Francisco: Harper & Row, 1996

The Partnership Way
New Tools for Living and Learning
With David Loye
Brandon, VT: Holistic Education Press, 1998

The Real Wealth of Nations
Creating a Caring Economics
San Francisco: Berrett-Koehler Publishers, 2008

Eliade, Mircea

Shamanism
Archaic Techniques of Ecstasy
New York: Pantheon Books, 1964

Ellis, Havelock

Sexual Inversion
Republished
New York: University Press of the Pacific, 2001
Originally published in 1897

Analysis of the Sexual Impulse
Love and Pain
The Sexual Impulse in Women
Republished
New York: University Press of the Pacific, 2001
Originally published in 1903

The Dance of Life
New York: Greenwood Press Reprint Edition, 1973
Originally published in 1923

Elwin, V.

The Muria and their Ghotul
Bombay: Oxford University Press, 1947

Emerson, Ralph Waldo

The Essays of Ralph Waldo Emerson
Cambridge, Mass.: Harvard University Press, 1987

Emoto, Masaru

The Hidden Messages in Water
New York: Atria Books, 2004

Die Botschaft des Wassers
Burgrain: Koha Verlag, 2008

The Secret Life of Water
New York: Atria Books, 2005

Die Heilkraft des Wassers
Burgrain: Koha Verlag, 2004

Encyclopédies d'Aujourd'hui

Encyclopédie de la Franc-Maçonnerie
Paris: Librairie Générale Française, 2000
(La Pochothèque)

Erickson, Milton H.

My Voice Will Go With You
The Teaching Tales of Milton H. Erickson
by Sidney Rosen (Ed.)
New York: Norton & Co., 1991

Complete Works 1.0, CD-ROM
New York: Milton H. Erickson Foundation, 2001

Erikson, Erik H.

Childhood and Society
New York: Norton, 1993
First published in 1950

Erman/Ranke

Ägypten und Ägyptisches Leben im Altertum
Hildesheim: Gerstenberg, 1981

Evans-Wentz, Walter Yeeling

The Fairy Faith in Celtic Countries
London: Frowde, 1911
Republished by Dover Publications
(Minneola, New York), 2002

F

Farson, Richard

Birthrights
A Bill of Rights for Children
Macmillan, New York, 1974

Feinberg, Joel

Harmless Wrongdoing
The Moral Limits of the Criminal Law, Vol. 4
New York: Oxford University Press, 1990

Fensterhalm, Herbert

Don't Say Yes When You Want to Say No
With Jean Bear
New York: Dell, 1980

Fericla, Josep M.

Al trasluz de la Ayahuasca
Antropología cognitiva, oniromancia y consciencias alternativas
Barcelona: La Liebre de Marzo, 2002

Finkelhor, David

Sexually Victimized Children
New York: Free Press, 1981

Finkelstein, Haim N. (Ed.)

The Collected Writings of Salvador Dali
Cambridge: Cambridge University Press, 1998

Flack, Audrey

Art & Soul
Notes on Creating
New York: E P Dutton, Reissue Edition, 1991

Forte, Robert (Ed.)

Entheogens and the Future of Religion
Council on Spiritual Practices, 2nd ed., 2000

Fortune, Mary M.

Sexual Violence
New York: Pilgrim Press, 1994

Foster/Freed

A Bill of Rights for Children
6 FAMILY LAW QUARTERLY 343 (1972)

Foucault, Michel

The History of Sexuality, Vol. I : The Will to Knowledge
London: Penguin, 1998
First published in 1976

The History of Sexuality, Vol. II : The Use of Pleasure
London: Penguin, 1998
First published in 1984

The History of Sexuality, Vol. III : The Care of Self
London: Penguin, 1998
First published in 1984

Fourcade, Jean-Michel

Analyse transactionnelle et bioénergie
Paris: Delarge, 1981

Foxwood, Orion

The Faery Teachings
Arcata, CA: R.J. Steward Books, 2007

Franz Anton Mesmer

Franz Anton Mesmer und die Geschichte des Mesmerismus
Beiträge zum internationalen wissenschaftlichen Symposium
anlässlich des 250. Geburtstages von Mesmer
Stuttgart, 1985

Freud, Anna

War and Children
London: 1943

Freud, Sigmund

Three Essays on the Theory of Sexuality
in: The Standard Edition of the Complete Psychological
Works of Sigmund Freud
London: Hogarth Press, 1953-54
Vol. 7, pp. 130 ff
(first published in 1905)

Drei Abhandlungen zur Sexualtheorie
Frankfurt/M: Fischer, 1991

The Interpretation of Dreams
New York: Avon, Reissue Edition, 1980
and in: The Standard Edition of the Complete Psychological
Works of Sigmund Freud , (24 Volumes) ed. by James Strachey
New York: W. W. Norton & Company, 1976

Die Traumdeutung
Frankfurt/M: Fischer, 2005

Totem and Taboo
New York: Routledge, 1999
Originally published in 1913

Totem und Tabu
Einige Übereinstimmungen im Seelenleben der Wilden und
der Neurotiker
Frankfurt/M: Fischer Verlag, 1972

Freund, Kurt

Assessment of Pedophilia
in: Cook, M. and Howells, K. (eds.)
Adult Sexual Interest in Children
Academic Press, London, 1980

Frisch, Max

Biedermann und die Brandstifter
München: Suhrkamp, 1996
Erstmals 1955 als Hörspiel veröffentlicht

Fromm, Erich

The Anatomy of Human Destructiveness
New York: Owl Book, 1992
Originally published in 1973

Anatomie der menschlichen Destruktivität
Berlin: Rowohlt, 1977

Escape from Freedom
New York: Owl Books, 1994
Originally published in 1941

Die Furcht vor der Freiheit
München: DTV Verlag, 1993

To Have or To Be
New York: Continuum International Publishing, 1996
Originally published in 1976

Haben oder Sein
Die seelischen Grundlagen einer neuen Gesellschaft
München: DTV Verlag, 2005

The Art of Loving
New York: HarperPerennial, 2000
Originally published in 1956

Die Kunst des Liebens
Berlin: Ullstein, 2005

G

Gates, Bill

The Road Ahead
New York, Penguin, 1996
(Revised Edition)

Gawain, Shakti

Creative Visualization
Use the Power of Your Imagination to Create What You Want
Novato, CA: New World Library, 1995

Creative Visualization Meditations (Reader)
Novato, CA: New World Library, 1997

Geldard, Richard

Remembering Heraclitus
New York: Lindisfarne Books, 2000

Gerber, Richard

A Practical Guide to Vibrational Medicine
Energy Healing and Spiritual Transformation
New York: Harper & Collins, 2001

Geller, Uri

The Mindpower Kit
Includes Book, Audiotape, Quartz Crystal And Meditation Circle
New York: Penguin, 1996

Gesell, Izzy

Playing Along
37 Group Learning Activities Borrowed from Improvisational Theater
Whole Person Associates, 1997

Ghiselin, Brewster (Ed.)

The Creative Process
Reflections on Invention in the Arts and Sciences
Berkeley: University of California Press, 1985
First published in 1952

Gibson, Ian

The Shameful Life of Salvador Dali
New York: Norton, 1998

Gil, David G.

Societal Violence and Violence in Families
in: David G. Gil, Child Abuse and Violence
New York: Ams Press, 1928

Gimbutas, Marija

The Language of the Goddess
London: Thames & Hudson, 2001

Glucksmann, André, Wolton, Thierry

Silence On Tue
Paris: Grasset, 1986

Goethe, Johann Wolfgang von

The Theory of Colors
New York: MIT Press, 1970
First published in 1810

Goethes Farbenlehre
Leipzig: Seemann-Henschel Verlag, 1998

Goldenstein, Joyce

Einstein: Physicist and Genius
(Great Minds of Science)
New York: Enslow Publishers, 1995

Goldman, Jonathan & Goldman, Andi

Tantra of Sound
Frequencies of Healing
Charlottesville: Hampton Roads, 2005

Tantra des Klanges
Mehr Liebe und Intimität in der Partnerschaft
Mit CD
Hanau: Amra Verlag, 2009

Healing Sounds

The Power of Harmonies
Rochester: Healing Arts Press, 2002

Klangheilung
Die Schöpferkraft des Obertongesangs
Hanau: Amra Verlag, 2008

Healing Sounds
Principles of Sound Healing
DVD, 90 min.
Sacred Mysteries, 2004

Goldstein, Jeffrey H.

Aggression and Crimes of Violence
New York, 1975

Goleman, Daniel

Emotional Intelligence
New York, Bantam Books, 1995

EQ. Emotionale Intelligenz
München: DTV Verlag, 1997

Goodwin, Matthew O.

The Complete Numerology Guide
New York: Red Wheel/Weiser, 1988

Gordon, Rosemary

Pedophilia: Normal and Abnormal
in: Kraemer, The Forbidden Love
London, 1976

Gordon Wasson, R.

The Road to Eleusis
Unveiling the Secret of the Mysteries
With Albert Hofmann, Huston Smith, Carl Ruck and Peter Webster
Berkeley, CA: North Atlantic Books, 2008

Goswami, Amit

The Self-Aware Universe
How Consciousness Creates the Material World
New York: Tarcher/Putnam, 1995

Das Bewusste Universum
Wie Bewusstsein die materielle Welt erschafft
Stuttgart: Lüchow Verlag, 2007

Gottlieb, Adam

Peyote and Other Psychoactive Cacti
Ronin Publishing, 2nd edition, 1997

Grant

Grant's Method of Anatomy
10th ed., by John V. Basmajian
Baltimore, London: Williams & Wilkins, 1980

Greene, Liz

Astrology of Fate
York Beach, ME: Red Wheel/Weiser, 1986

Saturn
A New Look at an Old Devil
York Beach, ME: Red Wheel/Weiser, 1976

The Astrological Neptune and the Quest for Redemption
Boston: Red Wheel Weiser, 1996

The Mythic Journey
With Juliet Sharman-Burke
The Meaning of Myth as a Guide for Life
New York: Simon & Schuster (Fireside), 2000

Die Mythische Reise
Die Bedeutung der Mythen als ein Führer durch das Leben
München: Atmosphären Verlag, 2004

The Mythic Tarot
With Juliet Sharman-Burke
New York: Simon & Schuster (Fireside), 2001
Originally published in 1986

Le Tarot Mythique
Une nouvelle approche du Tarot
Paris: Solar, 1988

The Luminaries
The Psychology of the Sun and Moon in the Horoscope
With Howard Sasportas
York Beach, ME: Red Wheel/Weiser, 1992

Sonne und Mond
Die Bedeutung der grossen Lichter in der Mythologie und im Horoskop
Saarbrücken: Neue Erde/Lentz, 2000

Greer, John Michael

Earth Divination, Earth Magic
A Practical Guide to Geomancy
New York: Llewellyn Publications, 1999

Grinspoon, Lester

Marihuana
The Forbidden Medicine
With James B. Bakalar
New Haven, CT: Yale University Press, 1997
First published in 1971

Groeben/Boeckh/Thiesing/Ehlermann

Kommentar zum EWG-Vertrag
Band 2, Dritte Auflage
Baden-Baden: Nomos, 1983

Grof, Stanislav

Ancient Wisdom and Modern Science
New York: State University of New York Press, 1984

Beyond the Brain
Birth, Death and Transcendence in Psychotherapy
New York: State University of New York, 1985

LSD: Doorway to the Numinous
The Groundbreaking Psychedelic Research into Realms of the
Human Unconscious
Rochester: Park Street Press, 2009

Psychologie transpersonnelle
Paris: Rocher, 1984

Realms of the Human Unconscious
Observations from LSD Research
New York: E.P. Dutton, 1976

The Cosmic Game
Explorations of the Frontiers of Human Consciousness
New York: State University of New York Press, 1998

The Holotropic Mind
The Three Levels of Human Consciousness
With Hal Zina Bennett
New York: HarperCollins, 1993

When the Impossible Happens
Adventures in Non-Ordinary Reality
Louisville, CO: Sounds True, 2005

Wir wissen mehr als unser Gehirn
Die Grenzen des Bewusstseins überschreiten
Freiburg: Herder, 2007

Groth, A. Nicholas

Men Who Rape
The Psychology of the Offender
New York: Perseus Publishing, 1980

Grout, Pam

Art & Soul
New York: Andrews McMeel Publishing, 2000

Gunn, John

Violence
New York/Washington, 1973

Gurdjieff, George Ivanovich

The Herald of Coming Good
London: Samuel Weiser, 1933

H

Hall, Manly P.

The Pineal Gland
The Eye of God
Article extracted from the book: Man the Grand Symbol of the Mysteries
Kessinger Publishing Reprint

The Secret Teachings of All Ages
Reader's Edition
New York: Tarcher/Penguin, 2003
Originally published in 1928

Hameroff, Newberg, Woolf, Bierman et al.

Consciousness
20 Scientists Interviewed
Director: Gregory Alsbury
5 DVD Box Set, 540 min.
New York: Alsbury Films, 2003

Hargous, Sabine

Les appeleurs d'âmes
L'univers chamanique des Indiens des Andes
Paris: Albin Michel, 1985

Harner, Michael

Ways of the Shaman
New York: Bantam, 1982
Originally published in 1980

Der Weg des Schamanen
Das praktische Grundlagenbuch zum Schamanismus
Genf: Ariston, 2007

Chamane
Les secrets d'un sorcier indien d'Amérique du Nord
Paris: Albin Michel, 1982

Hasegawa, Tsuyoshi

Racing the Enemy
Stalin, Truman, and the Surrender of Japan
Cambridge, MA: Belknap Press of Harvard University Press, 2006

Henkin/Pugh/Schachter/Smit

International Law
Cases and Materials
St. Paul (West): American Casebook Series, 1980

Herman, Dean M.

A Statutory Proposal to Prohibit the Infliction of Violence upon Children
19 FAMILY LAW QUARTERLY, 1986, 1-52

Hermes Trismegistos

Corpus Hermeticum
New York: Edaf, 2001

Héroard, J.

Journal de Jean Héroard sur l'Enfance et la Jeunesse de Louis XIII
Paris: Soulié/Barthélemy, 1868

Herrigel, Eugen

Zen in the Art of Archery
New York: Vintage Books, 1999
Originally published in 1971

Hicks, Esther and Jerry

The Amazing Power of Deliberate Intent
Living the Art of Allowing
Carlsbad, CA: Hay House, 2006

Hobbes, Thomas

Leviathan (1651)
New York: Longman Library, 2006

Hofmann, Albert

LSD, My Problem Child
Reflections on Sacred Drugs, Mysticism and Science
Santa Cruz, CA: Multidisciplinary Association for Psychedelic Studies,
2009
Originally published in 1980

LSD, Mein Sorgenkind
Die Entdeckung der 'Wunderdroge'
München: DTV Verlag, 1999

Holmes, Ernst

The Science of Mind
A Philosophy, A Faith, A Way of Life
New York: Jeremy P. Tarcher/Putnam, 1998
First Published in 1938

Holstiege, Hildegard

Montessori Pädagogik und soziale Humanität
Freiburg: Herder, 1994

Hood, J. X.

Scientific Curiosities of Love, Sex and Marriage
A Survey of Sex Relations, Beliefs and Customs of Mankind in
Different Countries and Ages
New York, 1951

Houston, Jean

The Possible Human
A Course in Enhancing Your Physical, Mental, and Creative Abilities
New York: Jeremy P. Tarcher/Putnam, 1982

Howells, Kevin

Adult Sexual Interest in Children
Considerations Relevant to Theories of Aetiology in:
Cook, M. and Howells, K. (eds.): Adult Sexual Interest in Children
Academic Press, London, 1980

Huang, Alfred

The Complete I Ching
The Definite Translation from Taoist Master Alfred Huang
Rochester, NY: Inner Traditions, 1998

Hunt, Valerie

Infinite Mind
Science of the Human Vibrations of Consciousness
Malibu, CA: Malibu Publishing, 2000

Huxley, Aldous

The Doors of Perception and Heaven and Hell
London: HarperCollins (Flamingo), 1994
(originally published in 1954)

The Perennial Philosophy
San Francisco: Harper & Row, 1970

I

Innocenti Declaration

Declaration on the Protection, Promotion and Support of Breastfeeding
http://www.innocenti15.net/inno.htm

J

Jackson, Nigel

The Rune Mysteries
With Silver RavenWolf
St. Paul, Minn.: Llewellyn Publications, 2000

Jackson, Stevi

Childhood and Sexuality
New York: Blackwell, 1982

Jaffe, Hans L.C.

Picasso
New York: Abradale Press, 1996

James, William

Writings 1902-1910
The Varieties of Religious Experience / Pragmatism / A Pluralistic
Universe / The Meaning of Truth / Some Problems of Philosophy / Essays
New York: Library of America, 1988

Jampolsky, Gerald

Aimer c'est se libérer de la peur
Genève: Éditions Soleil, 1986

Janov, Arthur

Primal Man
The New Consciousness
New York: Crowell, 1975

Das Neue Bewusstsein
Frankfurt/M: Fischer Verlag, 1988
Urausgabe 1975

Johnson, Paul

A History of the Jews
New York: Harper & Row, 1987

Johnston & Deisher

Contemporary Communal Child Rearing: A First Analysis
52 PEDIATRICS 319 (1973)

Jones, W.H.S., Litt, D.

Pliny Natural History
Cambridge, Mass.: Harvard University Press, 1980

Jung, Carl Gustav

Archetypen
München: DTV Verlag, 2001

Archetypes of the Collective Unconscious
in: The Basic Writings of C.G. Jung
New York: The Modern Library, 1959, 358-407

Collected Works
New York, 1959

Dialectique du moi et de l'inconscient
Paris, Gallimard, 1991

On the Nature of the Psyche
in: The Basic Writings of C.G. Jung
New York: The Modern Library, 1959, 47-133

Psychological Types
Collected Writings, Vol. 6
Princeton: Princeton University Press, 1971

Psychologie und Religion
München: DTV Verlag, 2001

Psychology and Religion
in: The Basic Writings of C.G. Jung
New York: The Modern Library, 1959, 582-655

Religious and Psychological Problems of Alchemy
in: The Basic Writings of C.G. Jung
New York: The Modern Library, 1959, 537-581

Symbol und Libido
Freiburg: Walter Verlag, 1987

Synchronizität, Akausalität und Okkultismus
Frankfurt/M: DTV, 2001

The Basic Writings of C.G. Jung
New York: The Modern Library, 1959

The Development of Personality
Collected Writings, Vol. 17
Princeton: Princeton University Press, 1954

The Meaning and Significance of Dreams
Boston: Sigo Press, 1991

The Myth of the Divine Child
in: Essays on A Science of Mythology
Princeton, N.J.: Princeton University Press Bollingen
Series XXII, 1969. (With Karl Kerenyi)

Traum und Traumdeutung
München: DTV Verlag, 2001

Two Essays on Analytical Psychology
Collected Writings, Vol. 7
Princeton: Princeton University Press, 1972
First published by Routledge & Kegan Paul, Ltd., 1953

Zur Psychologie westlicher und östlicher Religion
Fünfte Auflage
Olten: Walter Verlag, 1988

K

Kahn, Charles (Ed.)

The Art and Thought of Heraclitus
Cambridge: Cambridge University Press, 2008

Kaiser, Edmond

La Marche aux Enfants
Lausanne: P.-M. Favre, 1979

Kalweit, Holger

Shamans, Healers and Medicine Men
Boston and London: Shambhala, 1992
Originally published with Kösel Verlag, Munich, in 1987

Kant, Immanuel

Kant's Werke
Band VIII, Abhandlungen nach 1781 (Neudruck)
Berlin und Leipzig: Walter de Gruyter, 1923

Kapleau, Roshi Philip

Three Pillars of Zen
Boston: Beacon Press, 1967

Karagulla, Shafica

The Chakras
Correlations between Medical Science and Clairvoyant Observation
With Dora van Gelder Kunz
Wheaton: Quest Books, 1989

Die Chakras und die feinstofflichen Körper des Menschen
Mit Dora van Gelder-Kunz
Grafing: Aquamarin Verlag, 1994

Karremann, Manfred

Es geschieht am helllichten Tag
Die Verborgene Welt der Pädophilen
und wie wir unsere Kinder vor Missbrauch Schützen
Köln: Dumont, 2007

Kerner Justinus

F.A. Mesmer aus Schwaben
Frankfurt/M, 1856

Kiang, Kok Kok

The I Ching
An Illustrated Guide to the Chinese Art of Divination
Singapore: Asiapac, 1993

Kiesewetter, Carl

Franz Anton Mesmer's Leben und Lehre
Leipzig, 1893

Kingston, Karen

Creating Sacred Space With Feng Shui
New York: Broadway Books, 1997

Kinski, Klaus

Kinski Uncut: The Autobiography of Klaus Kinski
New York: Penguin, 1997

Klein, Melanie

Love, Guilt and Reparation, and Other Works 1921-1945
New York: Free Press, 1984
(Reissue Edition)

Envy and Gratitude and Other Works 1946-1963
New York: Free Press, 2002
(Reissue Edition)

Klimo, Jon

Channeling
Investigations on Receiving Information from Paranormal Sources
New York: North Atlantic Books, 1988

Koestler, Arthur

The Act of Creation
New York: Penguin Arkana, 1989.
Originally published in 1964

Kraemer

The Forbidden Love
London, 1976

Krafft-Ebing, Richard von

Psychopathia sexualis
New York: Bell Publishing, 1965
Originally published in 1886

Krause, Donald G.

The Art of War for Executives
London: Nicholas Brealey Publishing, 1995

Krishnamurti, J.

Freedom From The Known
San Francisco: Harper & Row, 1969

The First and Last Freedom
San Francisco: Harper & Row, 1975

Education and the Significance of Life
London: Victor Gollancz, 1978

Commentaries on Living
First Series
London: Victor Gollancz, 1985

Commentaries on Living
Second Series
London: Victor Gollancz, 1986
Krishnamurti's Journal
London: Victor Gollancz, 1987

Krishnamurti's Notebook
London: Victor Gollancz, 1986

Beyond Violence
London: Victor Gollancz, 1985

Beginnings of Learning
New York: Penguin, 1986

The Penguin Krishnamurti Reader
New York: Penguin, 1987

On God
San Francisco: Harper & Row, 1992

On Fear
San Francisco: Harper & Row, 1995

The Essential Krishnamurti
San Francisco: Harper & Row, 1996

The Ending of Time
With Dr. David Bohm
San Francisco: Harper & Row, 1985

Kwok, Man-Ho

The Feng Shui Kit
London: Piatkus, 1995

L

Labate, Beatriz Caluby

Ayahuasca Religions
A Comprehensive Bibliography and Critical Essays
Santa Cruz, CA: Maps, 2009

Laing, Ronald David

Divided Self
New York: Viking Press, 1991

R.D. Laing and the Paths of Anti-Psychiatry
ed., by Z. Kotowicz
London: Routledge, 1997

The Politics of Experience
New York: Pantheon, 1983

Sagesse, déraison et folie
Paris: Seuil, 1986

Lakhovsky, Georges

La Science et le Bonheur
Longévité et Immortalité par les Vibrations
Paris: Gauthier-Villars, 1930

Le Secret de la Vie
Paris: Gauthier-Villars, 1929

Secret of Life
New York: Kessinger Publishing, 2003

L'étiologie du Cancer
Paris: Gauthier-Villars, 1929

L'Universion
Paris: Gauthier-Villars, 1927

Lanouette, William

Genius in the Shadows
A Biography of Leo Szilard, the Man behind the Bomb
With Bela Silard
Chicago: University of Chicago Press, 1994

Laszlo, Ervin

Holos. Die Welt der neuen Wissenschaften
Petersberg: Via Nova Verlag, 2002

Science and the Akashic Field
An Integral Theory of Everything
Rochester: Inner Traditions, 2004

Macroshift
Die Herausforderung
Frankfurt/M: Insel Verlag, 2003

Quantum Shift to the Global Brain
How the New Scientific Reality Can Change Us and Our World
Rochester: Inner Traditions, 2008

Science and the Reenchantment of the Cosmos
The Rise of the Integral Vision of Reality
Rochester: Inner Traditions, 2006

The Akashic Experience
Science and the Cosmic Memory Field
Rochester: Inner Traditions, 2009

The Chaos Point
The World at the Crossroads
Newburyport, MA: Hampton Roads Publishing, 2006

Laud, Anne & Gilstrop, May

Violence in the Family
A Selected Bibliography on Child Abuse, Sexual Abuse of
Children & Domestic Violence
June 1985
University of Georgia Libraries
Bibliographical Series, No. 32

Lauterpacht, E., Q.C.

International Law Reports
Cambridge: Grotius Publishers

Lauterpacht, Hersch

International Law
Ed. By E. Lauterpacht, Q.C.
Vol. 3
London: Cambridge University Press, 1977

LaViolette, Paul A.

*Secrets of Antigravity Propulsion: Tesla, UFOs, and
Classified Aerospace Technology*
New York: Bear & Company, 2008

The U.S. Antigravity Squadron
In: Thomas Valone, Ed., *Electrogravitics Systems,
Reports on a New Propulsion Methodology*
Washington, D.C.: Integrity Research Institute, 1993, 78-96

Leadbeater, Charles Webster

Astral Plane
Its Scenery, Inhabitants and Phenomena
Kessinger Publishing Reprint Edition, 1997

Dreams
What they Are and How they are Caused
London: Theosophical Publishing Society, 1903
Kessinger Publishing Reprint Edition, 1998

The Inner Life
Chicago: The Rajput Press, 1911
Kessinger Publishing

Leary, Timothy

Our Brain is God
Berkeley, CA: Ronin Publishing, 2001
Author Copyright 1988

Über die Kriminalisierung des Natürlichen
Löhrbach: Werner Pieper Verlag, 1990

Leboyer, Frederick

Birth Without Violence
New York, 1975

Pour une Naissance sans Violence
Paris: Seuil, 1974

Geburt ohne Gewalt
München: Kösel 1981

Cette Lumière d'où vient l'Enfant
Paris: Seuil, 1978

Inner Beauty, Inner Light
New York: Newmarket Press, 1997

Weg des Lichts
München: Kösel, 1991

Loving Hands
The Traditional Art of Baby Massage
New York: Newmarket Press, 1977

Sanfte Hände
Die Kunst der indischen Baby-Massage
München: Kösel, 1979

The Art of Breathing
New York: Newmarket Press, 1991

Le Crapouillot

Les pédophiles
Nouvelle série, n°73, Janvier 1984
Vincent Acker, Le Vilain Manège du Coral, pp. 36-42

LeCron, Leslie M.

L'auto-hypnose
8e édition
Genève: Ariston, 1984

Leggett, Trevor P.

A First Zen Reader
Rutland: C.E. Tuttle, 1980
Originally published in 1972

Lenihan, Eddie

Meeting the Other Crowd
The Fairy Stories of Hidden Ireland
With Carolyn Eve Green
New York: Jeremy P. Tarcher/Penguin, 2004
Authors Copyright 2003

Leonard, George, Murphy, Michael

The Live We Are Given
A Long Term Program for Realizing the
Potential of Body, Mind, Heart and Soul
New York: Jeremy P. Tarcher/Putnam, 1984

Leopardi, Angelo (Hrsg.)

Der Pädosexuelle Komplex
Frankfurt/M: Foerster Verlag, 1988

Licht, Hans

Sexual Life in Ancient Greece
New York: AMS Press, 1995

Liedloff, Jean

Continuum Concept
In Search of Happiness Lost
New York: Perseus Books, 1986
First published in 1977

Auf der Suche nach dem verlorenen Glück
Gegen die Zerstörung der Glücksfähigkeit in der frühen Kindheit
München: C.H. Beck Verlag, 2006

Lip, Evelyn

The Design & Feng Shui of Logos, Trademarks and Signboards
Singapore: Prentice Hall, 1995

Lipgens, Walter

Europa-Föderationspläne der Widerstandsbewegungen 1940-1945
München, 1968

Lipton, Bruce

The Biology of Belief
Unleashing the Power of Consciousness, Matter and Miracles
Santa Rosa, CA: Mountain of Love/Elite Books, 2005

Intelligente Zellen
Wie Erfahrungen unsere Gene steuern
Burgrain: Koha Verlag, 2006

Liss, Jérôme

Débloquez vos émotions
Lausanne: Éditions Far, 1988

Locke, John

Some Thoughts Concerning Education
London, 1690
Reprinted in: The Works of John Locke, 1823
Vol. IX., pp. 6-205

Gedanken über Erziehung
Ditzingen: Reclam Verlag, 1986

Long, Max *Freedom*

The Secret Science at Work
The Huna Method as a Way of Life
Marina del Rey: De Vorss Publications, 1995
Originally published in 1953

Geheimes Wissen hinter Wundern
Die Entdeckung der HUNA-Lehre
Darmstadt: Schirner Verlag, 2006

Growing Into Light
A Personal Guide to Practicing the Huna Method,
Marina del Rey: De Vorss Publications, 1955

Lowen, Alexander

Angst vor dem Leben
Über den Ursprung seelischen Leides und den Weg zu
einem reicheren Dasein
München: Goldmann Wilhelm, 1989

Bioenergetics
New York: Coward, McGoegham 1975

Bioenergetik
Therapie der Seele durch Arbeit mit dem Körper
Berlin: Rowohlt, 2008

Depression and the Body
The Biological Basis of Faith and Reality
New York: Penguin, 1992

Fear of Life
New York: Bioenergetic Press, 2003

Honoring the Body
The Autobiography of Alexander Lowen
New York: Bioenergetic Press, 2004

Joy
The Surrender to the Body and to Life
New York: Penguin, 1995

Liebe und Orgasmus
Persönlichkeitserfahrung durch sexuelle Erfüllung
München: Goldmann Wilhelm, 1993

Love and Orgasm
New York: Macmillan, 1965

Love, Sex and Your Heart
New York: Bioenergetics Press, 2004

Narcissism: Denial of the True Self
New York: Macmillan, Collier Books, 1983

Narzissmus
Die Verleugnung des wahren Selbst
München: Goldmann Wilhelm, 1992

Pleasure: A Creative Approach to Life
New York: Bioenergetics Press, 2004
First published in 1970

The Language of the Body
Physical Dynamics of Character Structure
New York: Bioenergetics Press, 2006

Luna, Luis Eduardo & Amaringo, Pablo
Ayahuasca Visions
North Atlantic Books, 1999

Lusk, Julie T. (Editor)
30 Scripts for Relaxation Imagery & Inner Healing
Whole Person Associates, 1992

Lutyens, Mary
Krishnamurti: The Years of Fulfillment
New York: Avon Books, 1983

Krishnamurti: Die Biographie
München: Aquamarin Verlag, 1997

The Life and Death of Krishnamurti
Chennai: Krishnamurti Foundation India, 1990

Lutzbetak, Louis J.
Marriage and the Family in Caucasia
Vienna, 1951, first reprinting, 1966

M

Machiavelli, Niccolo
The Prince
New York: Soho Books, 2009
Written in 1513
First posthumous publishing 1531

Der Fürst
Frankfurt/M: Insel Verlag, 2009

Mack, Carol K. & Mack, Dinah
A Field Guide to Demons, Fairies, Fallen Angels, and Other Subversive Spirits
New York: Owl Books, 1998

Maharshi, Ramana
The Collected Works of Ramana Maharshi
New York: Sri Ramanasramam, 2002

The Essential Teachings of Ramana Maharshi
A Visual Journey
New York: Inner Directions Publishing, 2002
by Matthew Greenblad

Sei was du bist!
München: O.W. Barth, 2001

Nan Yar? Wer bin ich?
München: Kamphausen, 2002

Maisel, Eric

Fearless Creating
A Step-By-Step Guide to Starting and Completing
Work of Art
New York: Tarcher & Putnam, 1995

Malachi, Tau

Gnosis of the Cosmic Christ
A Gnostic Christian Kabbalah
St. Paul: Llewellyn Publications, 2005

Malinowski, Bronislaw

Crime und Custom in Savage Society
London: Kegan, 1926

Sex and Repression in Savage Society
London: Kegan, 1927

The Sexual Life of Savages in North West Melanesia
New York: Halycon House, 1929

Das Geschlechtsleben der Wilden in Nordwest-Melanesien
Liebe, Ehe und Familienleben bei den Eingeborenen
der Trobriand Inseln,
Britisch-Neuguinea
Eschborn: Klotz Verlag, 2005

Mallet, Carl-Heinz

Das Einhorn bin ich
Das Bild des Menschen im Märchen
Hamburg: Hoffmann & Campe Verlag, 1982

Untertan Kind
Nachforschungen über Erziehung
München: Max Hueber Verlag, 1987

Mann, Edward W.

Orgone, Reich & Eros
Wilhelm Reich's Theory of Life Energy
New York: Simon & Schuster (Touchstone), 1973

Mann, Sally

At Twelve
Portraits of Young Women
New York: Aperture, 1988

Immediate Family
New York: Phaidon Press, 1993

Marciniak, Barbara

Bringers of the Dawn
Teachings from the Pleiadians
New York: Bear & Co., 1992

Boten des Neuen Morgens
Lehren von den Pleiaden
Freiburg: Hermann Bauer Verlag, 1995

Martinson, Floyd M.

Sexual Knowledge
Values and Behavior Patterns
St. Peter: Minn.: Gustavus Adolphus College, 1966

Infant and Child Sexuality
St. Peter: Minn.: Gustavus Adolphus College, 1973

The Quality of Adolescent Experiences
St. Peter: Minn.: Gustavus Adolphus College, 1974

The Child and the Family
Calgary, Alberta: The University of Calgary, 1980

The Sex Education of Young Children
in: Lorna Brown (Ed.), *Sex Education in the Eighties*
New York, London: Plenum Press, 1981, pp. 51 ff.

The Sexual Life of Children
New York: Bergin & Garvey, 1994

Children and Sex, Part II: Childhood Sexuality
in: Bullough & Bullough, Human Sexuality (1994)
Pp. 111-116

Master Lam Kam Chuen
The Way of Energy
Mastering the Chinese Art of Internal
Strength with Chi Kung Exercise
New York: Simon & Schuster (Fireside), 1991

Master Liang, Shou-Yu & Wu, Wen-Ching
Tai Chi Chuan
24 & 48 Postures With Martial Applications
Roslindale, Mass.: YMAA Publication Center, 1996

Masters, R.E.L.
Forbidden Sexual Behavior and Morality
New York, 1962

McCarey, William A.

In Search of Healing
Whole-Body Healing Through the Mind-Body-Spirit Connection
New York: Berkley Publishing, 1996

McCormick

McCormick on Evidence
by Edward W. Cleary, 3d ed.
Lawyers Edition (Homebook Series)
St. Paul: West, 1984

McKenna, Terence

The Archaic Revival
San Francisco: Harper & Row, 1992

Food of The Gods
A Radical History of Plants, Drugs and Human Evolution
London: Rider, 1992

Die Speisen der Götter
Berlin: Synergia/Syntropia, 1996

The Invisible Landscape
Mind Hallucinogens and the I Ching
New York: HarperCollins, 1993
(With Dennis McKenna)

True Hallucinations
Being the Account of the Author's Extraordinary
Adventures in the Devil's Paradise
New York: Fine Communications, 1998

McLeod, Kembrew

Freedom of Expression
Resistance and Repression in the Age of Intellectual Property
Minneapolis, MN: University of Minnesota Press, 2007

McNiff, Shaun

Art as Medicine
Boston: Shambhala, 1992

Art as Therapy
Creating a Therapy of the Imagination
Boston/London: Shambhala, 1992

Trust the Process
An Artist's Guide to Letting Go
New York: Shambhala Publications, 1998

McTaggart, Lynne

The Field
The Quest for the Secret Force of the Universe
New York: Harper & Collins, 2002

Mead, Margaret

Sex and Temperament in Three Primitive Societies
New York, 1935

Meadows, Donella H.

Thinking in Systems
A Primer
White River, VT: Chelsea Green Publishing, 2008

Mehta, Rohit

J. Krishnamurti and the Nameless Experience
A Comprehensive Discussion of J. Krishnamurti's Approach to Life
Delhi: Motilal Banarsidass Publishers, 2002

Méric, de, Philippe

Le Yoga sans postures
Paris: Livre de Poche, 1967

Merle, Roger & Vitu, André
Traité de Croit Criminel
Droit Pénal Spécial
Vol. II, par André Vitu
Paris: Editions Cujas, 1982

Merleau-Ponty, Maurice
Phenomenology of Perception
London: Routledge, 1995
Originally published 1945

Phénoménologie de la perception
Paris: Gallimard, 1945

Metzner, Ralph (Ed.)
Ayahuasca, Human Consciousness and the Spirits of Nature
ed. by Ralph Metzner, Ph.D
New York: Thunder's Mouth Press, 1999

The Psychedelic Experience
A Manual Based on the Tibetan Book of the Dead
With Timothy Leary and Richard Alpert
New York: Citadel, 1995

Miller, Alice
Four Your Own Good
Hidden Cruelty in Child-Rearing and the Roots of Violence
New York: Farrar, Straus & Giroux, 1983

Am Anfang war Erziehung
München: Suhrkamp Verlag, 2008
Erstmals publiziert im Jahre 1986

Pictures of a Childhood
New York: Farrar, Straus & Giroux, 1986

The Drama of the Gifted Child
In Search for the True Self

translated by Ruth Ward
New York: Basic Books, 1996

Das Drama des Begabten Kindes
Und die Suche nach dem wahren Selbst
München: Suhrkamp Verlag, 1983

Der gemiedene Schlüssel
München: Suhrkamp, 2007

Das verbannte Wissen
Frankfurt/M: Suhrkamp, 1988

Thou Shalt Not Be Aware
Society's Betrayal of the Child
New York: Noonday, 1998

Du Sollst Nicht Merken
Variationen über das Paradies-Thema
Neuauflage
München: Suhrkamp, 2005

The Political Consequences of Child Abuse
in: The Journal of Psychohistory 26, 2 (Fall 1998)

Miller, Mary & Taube, Karl
An Illustrated Dictionary of the Gods and Symbols of Ancient Mexico and the Maya
London: Thames & Hudson, 1993

Moll, Albert
The Sexual Life of the Child
New York: Macmillan, 1912
First published in German as
Das Sexualleben des Kindes, 1909

Monroe, Robert
Ultimate Journey
New York: Broadway Books, 1994

Monsaingeon, Bruno

Svjatoslav Richter
Notebooks and Conversations
Princeton: Princeton University Press, 2002

Richter
Écrits, conversations
Paris: Éditions Van de Velde, 1998

Richter The Enigma / L'Insoumis / Der Unbeugsame
NVC Arts 1998 (DVD)

Montagu, Ashley

Touching
The Human Significance of the Skin
New York: Harper & Row, 1978

Körperkontakt
8. Auflage
Stuttgart: Klett/Cotta, 1995

Monter, E. William

Witchcraft in France and Switzerland
Ithaca & London: Cornell University Press, 1976

Montessori, Maria

The Absorbent Mind
Reprint Edition
New York: Buccaneer Books, 1995
First published in 1973

Das Kreative Kind
Der absorbierende Geist
Freiburg: Herder, 2007

Moody, Raymond

The Light Beyond
New York: Mass Market Paperback (Bantam), 1989

Moore, Thomas

Care of the Soul
A Guide for Cultivating Depth and Sacredness in Everyday Life
New York: Harper & Collins, 1994

Die Seele Lieben
Tiefe und Spiritualität im täglichen Leben
München: Droemer Knaur, 1995

Moser, Charles Allen

DSM-IV-TR and the Paraphilias: an argument for removal
With Peggy J. Kleinplatz
Journal of Psychology and Human Sexuality 17 (3/4), 91-109 (2005)

Murdock, G.

Social Structure
New York: Macmillan, 1960

Murphy, Joseph

The Power of Your Subconscious Mind
West Nyack, N.Y.: Parker, 1981, N.Y.: Bantam, 1982
Originally published in 1962

Die Macht Ihres Unterbewusstseins
München: Hugendubel, 2000

La puissance de votre subconscient
Genève: Ramón Keller, 1967

The Miracle of Mind Dynamics
New York: Prentice Hall, 1964

Miracle Power for Infinite Riches
West Nyack, N.Y.: Parker, 1972

The Amazing Laws of Cosmic Mind Power
West Nyack, N.Y.: Parker, 1973

Secrets of the I Ching
West Nyack, N.Y.: Parker, 1970

Think Yourself Rich
Use the Power of Your Subconscious Mind to Find True Wealth
Revised by Ian D. McMahan, Ph.D.
Paramus, NJ: Reward Books, 2001

Das Erfolgsbuch
Wie sie alles im Leben erreichen können
Hamburg: Heyne Verlag, 2002

Wahrheiten die ihr Leben verändern
Dr. Joseph Murphys Vermächtnis
München: Hugendubel, 1996

Murphy, Michael

The Future of the Body
Explorations into the Further Evolution of Human Nature
New York: Jeremy P. Tarcher/Putnam, 1992

Der Quanten-Mensch
München: Ludwig Verlag, 1996

Myers, Tony Pearce

The Soul of Creativity
Insights into the Creative Process
Novato, CA: New World Library, 1999

Myss, Caroline

The Creation of Health
The Emotional, Psychological, and Spiritual Responses that Promote
Health and Healing
New York: Three Rivers Press, 1998

N

Naparstek, Belleruth

Your Sixth Sense
Unlocking the Power of Your Intuition
London: HarperCollins, 1998

Staying Well With Guided Imagery
New York: Warner Books, 1995

Narby, Jeremy

The Cosmic Serpent
DNA and the Origins of Knowledge
New York: J. P. Tarcher, 1999

Die Kosmische Schlange
Auf den Pfaden der Schamanen zu den Ursprüngen modernen Wissens
Stuttgart: Klett-Cotta, 2007

Nau, Erika

Self-Awareness Through Huna
Virginia Beach: Donning, 1981

Selbstbewusst durch Huna
Die magische Weisheit Hawaiis
2. Auflage
Basel: Sphinx Verlag, 1989

Neill, Alexander Sutherland

Neill! Neill! Orange-Peel!
New York: Hart Publishing Co., 1972

Neill! Neill! Birnenstiel!
Berlin: Rowohlt, 1973

Summerhill
A Radical Approach to Child Rearing
New York: Hart Publishing, Reprint 1984
Originally published 1960

Theorie und Praxis der Antiautoritären Erziehung
Das Beispiel Summerhill
Berlin: Rowohlt Verlag, 1969

Summerhill School
A New View of Childhood
New York: St. Martin's Press
Reprint 1995

Das Prinzip Summerhill
Berlin: Rowohlt, 1971

Neuhaus, Heinrich

The Art of Piano Playing
London: Barrie & Jenkins, 1973
Reprinted 1997, 2001, 2002, 2006
First published in 1958

Neumann, Erich

The Great Mother
Princeton: Princeton University Press, 1955
(Bollingen Series)

Die Grosse Mutter
Die weiblichen Gestaltungen des Unterbewussten
Düsseldorf: Patmos Verlag, 2003

Newton, Michael
Life Between Lives
Hypnotherapy for Spiritual Regression
Woodbury, Minn.: Llewellyn Publications, 2006

Ni, Hua-Ching
I Ching
The Book of Changes and the Unchanging Truth
2nd edition
Santa Barbara: Seven Star Communications, 1999

Esoteric Tao The Ching
The Shrine of the Eternal Breath of Tao
Santa Monica: College of Tao and Traditional
Chinese Healing, 1992

The Complete Works of Lao Tzu
Tao The Ching & Hua Hu Ching
Translation and Elucidation by Hua-Ching Ni
Santa Monica: Seven Star Communications, 1995

Nichols, Sallie
Jung and Tarot: An Archetypal Journey
New York: Red Wheel/Weiser, 1986

Die Psychologie des Tarot
Interlaken: Ansata Verlag, 1996

Nin, Anaïs
The Diary of Anaïs Nin (7 Volumes)
New York, 1966

Volume 1 (1931-1934)
New York: Harvest Books, 1969

Volume 2 (1934-1939)
New York: Harvest Books, 1970

O

O'Brian, Shirley

Child Pornography
2nd edition
New York: Kendall/Hunt, 1992

Odent, Michel

Birth Reborn
What Childbirth Should Be
London: Souvenir Press, 1994

The Scientification of Love
London: Free Association Books, 1999

Die Wurzeln der Liebe
Wie unsere wichtigsten Emotionen entstehen
Olten: Walter Verlag, 2001

Primal Health
Understanding the Critical Period Between Conception
and the First Birthday
London: Clairview Books, 2002
First Published in 1986 with Century Hutchinson in London

La Santé Primale
Paris: Payot, 1986

Die sanfte Geburt
Die Leboyer-Methode in der Praxis
Bergisch-Gladbach: Lübbe Verlag, 2001

The Functions of the Orgasms
The Highway to Transcendence
London: Pinter & Martin, 2009

Ollendorf-Reich, Ilse

Wilhelm Reich, A Personal Biography
New York, St. Martins Press, 1969

Wilhelm Reich
Vorwort von A.S. Neill
München, Kindler, 1975

Ong, Hean-Tatt

Amazing Scientific Basis of Feng-Shui
Kuala Lumpur: Eastern Dragon Press, 1997

Oppenheim, Lassa

International Law
4th Edition, by Sir Arnold D. McNair
New York, 1928

Ostrander, Sheila & Schroeder, Lynn

Superlearning 2000
New York: Delacorte Press, 1994

Superlearning
Die revolutionäre Lernmethode
München: Scherz Verlag, 1979

Supermemory
New York: Carroll & Graf, 1991

SuperMemory
Der Weg zum optimalen Gedächtnis
München: Goldmann, 1996

Ouspensky, Pyotr Demianovich

In Search of the Miraculous
New York: Mariner Books, 2001
First published in 1949

P

Papus

(Dr Gérard Encausse)
Traité de Magique Pratique
16e édition
St. Jean de Braye: Éditions Dangles, 1989

Patridge, Burgo

History of Orgies
New York, 1960

Pearce, John A. II and Robinson B. Jr.

Strategic Management
Formulation, Implementation and Control
Tenth Edition
New York: McGraw-Hill, 2007

Pearce Myers, Tony (Editor)

The Soul of Creativity
Insights into the Creative Process
Novato: New World Library, 1999

Pert, Candace B.

Molecules of Emotion
The Science Behind Mind-Body Medicine
New York: Scribner, 2003

Petrash, Jack

Understanding Waldorf Education
Teaching from the Inside Out
London: Floris Books, 2003

Phipson

Phipson on Evidence
13th ed., by John Huxley Buzzard
Richard May and M. N. Howard
London: Sweet & Maxwell, 1982

Plato

Complete Works
Ed. by John M. Cooper
New York: Hackett Publishing Company, 1997

Plummer, Kenneth

Pedophilia
Constructing a Sociological Baseline
in: in: Cook, M. and Howells, K. (Eds.):
Adult Sexual Interest in Children
Academic Press, London, 1980, pp. 220 ff.

Plutarch

Plutarch's Lives
The Dryden Translation
New York: Bantam Books, 2006

Ponder, Catherine

The Healing Secrets of the Ages
Marine del Rey: DeVorss, 1985

Porteous, Hedy S.

Sex and Identity
Your Child's Sexuality
Indianapolis: Bobbs-Merrill, 1972

Prescott, James W.

Affectional Bonding for the Prevention of Violent Behaviors
Neurobiological, Psychological and Religious/Spiritual Determinants
in: Hertzberg, L.J., Ostrum, G.F. and Field, J.R., (Eds.)

Violent Behavior
Vol. 1, Assessment & Intervention, Chapter Six
New York: PMA Publishing, 1990

Alienation of Affection
Psychology Today, December 1979

Body Pleasure and the Origins of Violence
Bulletin of the Atomic Scientists, 10-20 (1975)

Deprivation of Physical Affection as a Primary Process in the
Development of Physical Violence A Comparative
and Cross-Cultural Perspective,
in: David G. Gil, ed., Child Abuse and Violence
New York: Ams Press, 1979

Early somatosensory deprivation as an ontogenetic
process in the abnormal development of the brain and behavior,
in: Medical Primatology, ed. by I.E. Goldsmith and J. Moor-Jankowski,
New York: S. Karger, 1971

Genital Mutilation of Children
Failure of Humanity and Humanism
Unprinted Essay (2005)
http://www.violence.de/prescott/letters/
CIRC_CONGRESS_MONTAGUE_9.30.05.html

Genital Pain vs. Genital Pleasure
Why the One and not the Other
The Truth Seeker, July/August 1989, pp. 14-21
http://www.violence.de/prescott/truthseeker/genpl.html

How Culture Shapes the Developing Brain and the Future of Humanity
A Brief Summary of the research which links brain
abnormalities and violence to an absence of nurturing and bonding
very early in childhood,
in: Touch the Future: Optimum Learning Relationships
for Children & Adults
Spring 2002 (Ed. by Michael Mendizza)
Nevada City, CA, 2002

Invited Commentary: Central nervous system functioning in altered sensory environments,
in: M.H. Appley and R. Trumbull (Eds.), *Psychological Stress*,
New York: Appleton-Century Crofts, 1967

Our Two Cultural Brains: Neurointegrative and Neurodissociative
http://www.violence.de/prescott/letters/Our_Two_Cultural_Brains.pdf

Phylogenetic and ontogenetic aspects of human affectional development,
in: Progress in Sexology, Proceedings of the 1976 International Congress of Sexology,
ed. by R. Gemme & C.C. Wheeler
New York: Plenum Press, 1977

Prevention or Therapy and the Politics of Trust
Inspiring a New Human Agenda
in: *Psychotherapy and Politics International*
Volume 3(3), pp. 194-211
London: John Wiley, 2005

Sex and the Brain
Midcontinent & Eastern Regions, June 13-16, 2002
Big Rapids, MI: Society for Cross-Cultural Research,
32nd Annual Meeting, 2005
http://www.violence.de/archive.shtml

Sixteen Principles for Personal, Family and Global Peace
The Truth Seeker, March/April 1989
http://www.violence.de/prescott/letters/Sixteen_Principles.pdf

Somatosensory affectional deprivation (SAD) theory of drug and alcohol use,
in: Theories on Drug Abuse: Selected Contemporary Perspectives,
ed. by Dan J. Lettieri, Mollie Sayers and Helen Wallenstien Pearson,
NIDA Research Monograph 30, March 1980
Rockville, MD: National Institute on Drug Abuse,
Department of Health and Human Services, 1980

The Origins of Human Love and Violence
Pre- and Perinatal Psychology Journal
Volume 10, Number 3:
Spring 1996, pp. 143-188The Origins of Love and Violence
Sensory Deprivation and the Developing Brain
Research and Prevention (DVD)
http://ttfuture.org/store/origins_orders

http://violence.de
http://ttfuture.org/violence
http://montagunocircpetition.org

Pritchard, Colin

The Child Abusers
New York: Open University Press, 2004

R

Radin, Dean

The Conscious Universe
The Scientific Truth of Psychic Phenomena
San Francisco: Harper & Row, 1997

Entangled Minds
Extrasensory Experiences in a Quantum Reality
New York: Paraview Pocket Books, 2006

Raknes, Ola

Wilhelm Reich and Orgonomy
Oslo: Universitetsforlaget, 1970

Wilhelm Reich und die Orgonomie
Eine Einführung in die Wissenschaft von der Lebensenergie
Frankfurt/M: Nexus, 1983

Randall, Neville

Life After Death
London: Robert Hale, 1999

Rank, Otto

Art and Artist
With Charles Francis Atkinson and Anaïs Nin
New York: W.W. Norton, 1989
Originally published in 1932

The Significance of Psychoanalysis for the Mental Sciences
New York: BiblioBazaar, 2009
First published in 1913

Rausky, Franklin

Mesmer ou la révolution thérapeutique
Paris, 1977

Redfield, James

The Tenth Insight
Holding the Vision
New York: Warner Books, 1996

The Celestine Prophecy
New York: Warner Books, 1995

Die Vision von Celestine
Berlin: Ullstein, 2004

Reich, Wilhelm

*A Review of the Theories, dating from The 17th Century,
on the Origin of Organic Life*
by Arthur Hahn, Literature Assistant at the Institut für
Sexualökonomische Lebensforschung, Biologisches Laboratorium,
Oslo, 1938
©1979 Mary Boyd Higgins as Director of the Wilhelm Reich Infant Trust
XEROX Copy from the Wilhelm Reich Museum

Children of the Future
On the Prevention of Sexual Pathology
New York: Farrar, Straus & Giroux, 1984
First published in 1950

CORE (Cosmic Orgone Engineering)
Part I, Space Ships, DOR and DROUGHT
©1984, Orgone Institute Press
XEROX Copy from the Wilhelm Reich Museum

Der Einbruch der sexuellen Zwangsmoral
Frankfurt/M: Fischer, 1981

Die Entdeckung des Orgons II
Der Krebs
Frankfurt/M: Fischer, 1981
Köln: Kiepenheuer & Witsch, 1984

Die Funktion des Orgasmus
Sexualökonomische Grundprobleme der biologischen Energie
Köln: Kiepenheuer & Witsch, 1987

Die Massenpsychologie des Faschismus
Frankfurt/M: Fischer, 1974

Die sexuelle Revolution
Frankfurt/M: Fischer, 1966

Early Writings 1
New York: Farrar, Straus & Giroux, 1975

Ether, God & Devil & Cosmic Superimposition
New York: Farrar, Straus & Giroux, 1972
Originally published in 1949

Frühe Schriften 1
Aus den Jahren 1920-1925
Frankfurt/M: Fischer, 1983

Frühe Schriften 2
Genitalität in der Theorie und Therapie der Neurose
Frankfurt/M: Fischer, 1985

Genitality in the Theory and Therapy of Neurosis
©1980 by Mary Boyd Higgins as Director of the Wilhelm Reich
Infant Trust

Leidenschaften der Jugend
Köln: Kiepenheuer & Witsch, 1984

L'irruption de la morale sexuelle
Paris: Payot, 1972

Menschen im Staat
Frankfurt/M: Nexus, 1982

People in Trouble
©1974 by Mary Boyd Higgins as Director of the Wilhelm Reich
Infant Trust

Record of a Friendship
The Correspondence of Wilhelm Reich and A. S. Neill
New York, Farrar, Straus & Giroux, 1981

Selected Writings
An Introduction to Orgonomy
New York: Farrar, Straus & Giroux, 1973

The Bioelectrical Investigation of Sexuality and Anxiety
New York: Farrar, Straus & Giroux, 1983
Originally published in 1935

The Bion Experiments
reprinted in *Selected Writings*
New York: Farrar, Straus & Giroux, 1973

The Cancer Biopathy (The Orgone, Vol. 2)
New York: Farrar, Straus & Giroux, 1973

The Function of the Orgasm (The Orgone, Vol. 1)
Orgone Institute Press, New York, 1942

The Invasion of Compulsory Sex Morality
New York: Farrar, Straus & Giroux, 1971
Originally published in 1932

The Leukemia Problem: Approach
©1951, Orgone Institute Press
Copyright Renewed 1979
XEROX Copy from the Wilhelm Reich Museum

The Mass Psychology of Fascism
New York: Farrar, Straus & Giroux, 1970
Originally published in 1933

The Orgone Energy Accumulator
Its Scientific and Medical Use
©1951, 1979, Orgone Institute Press
XEROX Copy from the Wilhelm Reich Museum

The Schizophrenic Split
©1945, 1949, 1972 by Mary Boyd Higgins as Director of the
Wilhelm Reich Infant Trust
XEROX Copy from the Wilhelm Reich Museum

The Sexual Revolution
©1945, 1962 by Mary Boyd Higgins as Director of the
Wilhelm Reich Infant Trust

Zeugnisse einer Freundschaft
Der Briefwechsel zwischen Wilhelm Reich und A.S.
Neill (1936-1957)
Köln: Kiepenheuer & Witsch, 1986

Reid, Daniel P.
The Tao of Health, Sex & Longevity
A Modern Practical Guide to the Ancient Way
New York: Simon & Schuster, 1989

Guarding the Three Treasures
The Chinese Way of Health
New York: Simon & Schuster, 1993

Renault, Mary

The Persian Boy
New York: Bantam Books, 1972

Reps, Paul

Zen Flesh, Zen Bones
Rutland: Tuttle Publishing, 1989

Rhodes, Richard

The Making of the Atomic Bomb
New York, Simon & Schuster, 1995

Richardson, Justin

Everything You Never Wanted Your Kids to Know About Sex
With Mark. A. Schuster
New York: Three Rivers Press, 2003

Richet, Charles

Metapsychical Phenomena
Methods and Observations
Kessinger Publishing Reprint Edition, 2004
Originally published in 1905

Riso, Don Richard & Hudson, Russ

The Wisdom of the Enneagram
The Complete Guide to Psychological and Spiritual Growth
For The Nine Personality Types
New York: Bantam Books, 1999

Robbins, Anthony

Awaken The Giant Within
New York: Simon & Schuster, 1991

Unlimited Power
The New Science of Personal Achievement
New York: Free Press, 1997

Roberts, Jane

The Nature of Personal Reality
New York: Amber-Allen Publishing, 1994
First published in 1974

Die Natur der Persönlichen Realität
Ein neues Bewusstsein als Quelle der Kreativität
München: Kailash Verlag, 2007

The Nature of the Psyche
Its Human Expression
New York, Amber-Allen Publishing, 1996
First published in 1979

Die Natur der Psyche
Ihr menschlicher Ausdruck in Kreativität, Liebe, Sexualität
Genf: Ariston Verlag, 1985

Die Natur der Psyche
Ihr menschlicher Ausdruck in Kreativität, Liebe, Sexualität
München: Kailash Verlag, 2008

Roman, Sanaya

Opening to Channel
How To Connect With Your Guide
New York: H.J. Kramer, 1987

Zum Höheren Selbst Erwachen
Das Herz dem Bewusstsein des Lichts öffnen
Genf: Ansata Verlag, 2003

Rosen, Sydney (Ed.)

My Voice Will Go With You
The Teaching Tales of Milton H. Erickson
New York: Norton & Co., 1991

Rosenbaum, Julius

The Plague of Lust
New York: Frederick Publications, 1955

Rossman, Parker

Sexual Experiences between Men and Boys
New York, 1976

Rothschild & Wolf

Children of the Counterculture
New York: Garden City, 1976

Rousseau, Jean-Jacques

Émile ou de l'Éducation, 1762
Reprint, Paris: Garnier, 1964

The Social Contract
And Later Political Writings
Cambridge, MA.: Cambridge University Press, 1997

Rudhyar, Dane

Astrology of Personality
A Reformulation of Astrological Concepts and Ideals in
Terms of Contemporary Psychology and Philosophy
New York: Aurora Press, 1990

An Astrological Triptych
Gifts of the Spirit, The Way Through, and The Illumined Road
New York: Aurora Press, 1991

Astrological Mandala
New York: Vintage Books, 1994

L'astrologie de la transformation
Paris: Rocher, 1984

Ruiz, Don Miguel

The Four Agreements
A Practical Guide to Personal Freedom
San Rafael, CA: Amber Allen Publishing, 1997

The Mastery of Love
A Practical Guide to the Art of Relationship
San Rafael, CA: Amber Allen Publishing, 1999

The Voice of Knowledge
A Practical Guide to Inner Peace
With Janet Mills
San Rafael, CA: Amber Allen Publishing, 2004

Ruperti, Alexander

Cycles of Becoming
The Planetary Pattern of Growth
New York: CRCS Publications, 1978

La roue de l'expérience individuelle
Paris: Librairie de Médicis, 1991

Rush, Florence

The Best Kept Secret
Sexual Abuse of Children
New Jersey: Prentice-Hall, 1980

Das bestgehütete Geheimnis
Sexueller Kindesmissbrauch
Berlin: Sub-Rosa Frauenverlag, 1984

S

Saint-Simon, Claude-Henri de

De la réorganisation de la société européenne
Avec Auguste Thierry
Paris, 1814
Lausanne: Centre de Recherches Européennes, 1967

Salas, Floyd

Tatoo the Wicked Cross
New York: Grove Press, 1967

Salomé, Jacques

Si je m'écoutais, je m'entendrais
Avec Sylvie Galland
Paris: Éditions de l'Homme, 1990

Sandfort, Theo

The Sexual Aspect of Pedophile Relations
The Experience of Twenty-five Boys
Amsterdam: Pan/Spartacus, 1982

SantoPietro, Nancy

Feng Shui, Harmony by Design
How to Create a Beautiful and Harmonious Home,
New York: Putnam-Berkeley, 1996

Satinover, Jeffrey

Homosexuality and the Politics of Truth
New York: Baker Books, 1996

The Quantum Brain
New York: Wiley & Sons, 2001

Satprem

Sri Aurobindo ou l'aventure de la conscience
Paris: Buchet/Castel, 1970

Scarro A. M., Jr. (Ed.)

Male Rape
New York: Ams Press, 1982

Schérer, René

Co-ire
Album systématique de l'enfance
Avec Guy Hocquenghem
Recherches No. 22
Paris: E.S.F., 1976

Émile perverti, ou des rapports entre l'éducation et la sexualité
Paris: Robert Laffont, 1974
Paris, Désordres, 2006
Nouvelle Édition

Le corps interdit
Avec Georges Lapassade
Paris: E.S.F., 1976

Une érotique puérile
Paris: Éditions Galilée, 1978

Schlipp, Paul A. (Ed.)

Albert Einstein
Philosopher-Scientist
New York: Open Court Publishing, 1988

Schonberg, Harold

The Great Pianists
From Mozart to the Present
New York: Simon and Schuster (Fireside), 2006
Originally published in 1963

Schrenck-Notzing, Albert von

Phenomena of Materialization
A Contribution to the Investigation of Mediumistic Teleplastics
Perspectives in Psychical Research
New York: Kegan Paul, 1920

Schultes, Richard Evans, et al.

Plants of the Gods
Their Sacred, Healing, and Hallucinogenic Powers
New York: Healing Arts Press
2nd edition, 2002

Die Pflanzen der Götter
Die magischen Kräfte der Rausch- und Giftgewächse
München: AT Verlag, 1998

Schumacher, E.F.

Small is Beautiful
Economics as if People Mattered
San Francisco: Harper Perennial, 1989

Schwartz, Andrew E.

Guided Imagery for Groups
Fifty Visualizations That Promote Relaxation, Problem-Solving,
Creativity, and Well-Being
Whole Person Associates, 1995

Senf, Bernd

Die Wiederentdeckung des Lebendigen
Aachen: Omega, 2003
Erstmals veröffentlicht 1996 mit Zweitausendeins Verlag in Frankfurt/M

Nach Reich: Neue Forschungen zur Orgonenergie
Sexualökonomie / Die Entdeckung der Orgonenergie
Herausgegeben zusammen mit Professor James DeMeo,
Ashland, Oregon, USA
Frankfurt/M: Zweitausendeins Verlag, 1997

Sepper, Dennis L.

Goethe Contra Newton
Polemics and the Project of a New Science of Color
Cambridge: Cambridge University Press, 1988

Shalabi, Ahmad

Islam
Cairo, 1970

Sharaf, Myron

Fury on Earth
A Biography of Wilhelm Reich
London: André Deutsch, 1983

Wilhelm Reich
Der heilige Zorn des Lebendigen
Berlin: Simon & Leutner, 1994

Sheldrake, Rupert

A New Science of Life
The Hypothesis of Morphic Resonance
Rochester: Park Street Press, 1995

Das Schöpferische Universum
Die Theorie des morphogenetischen Feldes
Neue und erweiterte Auflage
Berlin: Ullstein, 2009

Sher, Barbara & Gottlieb, Annie

Wishcraft
How to Get What You Really Want
2nd edition
New York: Ballantine Books, 2003

Shone, Ronald

Creative Visualization
Using Imagery and Imagination for Self-Transformation
New York: Destiny Books, 1998

Simonton, O. Carl et al.

Getting Well Again
Los Angeles: Tarcher, 1978

Singer, June

Androgyny
New York: Doubleday Dell, 1976

Smith, C. Michael

Jung and Shamanism in Dialogue
London: Trafford Publishing, 2007

Spiller, Jan

Astrology for the Soul
New York: Bantam, 1997

Spock, Benjamin

Dr. Spock's Baby and Child Care
8th Edition
New York: Pocket Books, 2004

Säuglings- und Kinderpflege
Berlin: Ullstein, 1986

Spretnak, Charlene

Green Politics
Rochester, VT: Inner Traditions, 1986

Stein, Robert M.

Redeeming the Inner Child in Marriage and Therapy
in: Reclaiming the Inner Child
ed. by Jeremiah Abrams
New York: Tarcher/Putnam, 1990, 261 ff.

Steiner, Rudolf

Theosophy
An Introduction to the Spiritual Processes in Human Life
and in the Cosmos
New York: Anthroposophic Press, 1994

Die Erziehung des Kindes
Dornach: Rudolf Steiner Verlag, 2003
First published in 1907

Stekel, Wilhelm

Auto-Eroticism
A Psychiatric Study of Onanism and Neurosis
Republished, London: Paul Kegan, 2004

Patterns of Psychosexual Infantilism
New York, 1959 (reprint edition)

Psychosexueller Infantilismus
Die seelischen Kinderkrankheiten der Erwachsenen
Berlin: Urban & Schwarzenberg, 1922

Sadism and Masochism
New York: W.W. Norton & Co., 1953

Sex and Dreams
The Language of Dreams
Republished
New York: University Press of the Pacific, 2003

Störungen des Trieb- und Affektlebens
Bände I & II
Berlin: Urban & Schwarzenberg, 1921

Stiene, Bronwen & Frans

The Reiki Sourcebook
New York: O Books, 2003

The Japanese Art of Reiki
A Practical Guide to Self-Healing
New York: O Books, 2005

Stone, Hal & Stone, Sidra

Embracing Our Selves
The Voice Dialogue Manual
San Rafael, CA: New World Library, 1989

Du bist viele
Das 100fache Selbst und seine Entdeckung durch
die Voice-Dialogue Methode
München: Heyne Verlag, 1994

Strassman, Rick

DMT: The Spirit Molecule
A doctor's revolutionary research into the biology of near-death
and mystical experiences
Rochester: Park Street Press, 2001

Stratenwerth, Günter

Schweizerisches Strafrecht
Besonderer Teil II, 3. Aufl.
Bern: Stämpfli, 1984

Sun Tzu (Sun Tsu)

The Art of War
Special Edition
New York: El Paso Norte Press, 2007

Die Kunst des Krieges
Hamburg: Nikol Verlag, 2008

Suryani, Luh Ketut & Jensen, Gorden D.

The Balinese People
A Reinvestigation of Character
New York: Oxford University Press, 1993

Sutherland

Statutory Construction
Ed. By Sands, 4th Edition
London, 1975

Sweeny/Oliver/Leech

The International Legal System
Cases and Materials
2nd Edition
Minneola, N.Y.: Foundation Press, 1981

Symonds, John Addington

A Problem in Greek Ethics
New York: M.S.G. House, 1971

Szasz, Thomas

The Myth of Mental Illness
New York: Harper & Row, 1984

T

Talbot, Michael

The Holographic Universe
New York: HarperCollins, 1992

Das holographische Universum
Die Welt in neuer Dimension
München: Droemer Knaur, 1994

Tansley, David V.

Chakras, Rays and Radionics
London: Daniel Company Ltd., 1984

Targ, Russell & Katra, Jane

Miracles of Mind
Exploring Nonlocal Consciousness and Spiritual Healing
Novato, CA: New World Library, 1999

Tarnas, Richard

Cosmos and Psyche
Intimations of a New World View
New York: Plume, 2007

The Passion of the Western Mind
Understanding the Ideas that have Shaped Our World View
New York: Ballantine Books, 1993

Tart, Charles T.

Altered States of Consciousness
A Book of Readings
Hoboken, N.J.: Wiley & Sons, 1969

Tatar, Maria M.

Spellbound: Studies on Mesmerism and Literature
Princeton, N.Y., 1978

Tchouang-tseu

Oeuvre complète
Paris: Gallimard/Unesco, 1969

Temple, Robert

The Sirius Mystery
New Scientific Evidence of Alien Contact 5000 Years Ago
Rochester: Destiny Books, 1998

Textor, R. B.

A Cross-Cultural Summary
New Haven, Human Relations Area Files (HRAF)
Press, 1967

The Advent of Great Awakening

A Course in Miracles
Text Workbook and Manual for Teachers
New York: New Christian Church of Full Endeavor, 2007

The Tibetan Book of the Dead

The Great Liberation through Hearing in the Bardo
Translated with commentary by Francesca
Fremantle & Chögyam Trungpa
Boston: Shambhala Dragon Editions, 1975

The Ultimate Picasso

New York: Harry N. Abrams, 2000

Thorsson, Edred

Futhark
A Handbook of Rune Magic
San Francisco: Weiser Books, 1984

Tiller, William A.

Conscious Acts of Creation
The Emergence of a New Physics
Associated Producers, 2004 (DVD)

Psychoenergetic Science
New York: Pavior, 2007

Conscious Acts of Creation
New York: Pavior, 2001

Tischner, Rudolf

F.A. Mesmer
München, 1928

Todaro-Franceschi, Vidette

The Enigma of Energy
Where Science and Religion Converge
New York: Crossroad Publishing, 1991

Toffler, Alvin

Powershift
Knowledge, Wealth, and Violence at the Edge of the 21st Century
New York: Bantam, 1991

Revolutionary Wealth
How it will be created and how it will change our lives
New York: Broadway Business, 2007

The Third Wave
New York: Bantam, 1984

Tolle, Eckhart

The Power of Now
A Guide to Spiritual Enlightenment
Novato, CA: New World Library, 2004

Jetzt! Die Kraft der Gegenwart
Ein Leitfaden zum spirituellen Erwachen
Bielefeld: Kamphausen Verlag, 2000

A New Earth
Awakening to Your Life's Purpose
New York: Michael Joseph (Penguin), 2005

Eine neue Erde
Bewusstseinssprung anstelle von Selbstzerstörung
München: Goldmann, 2005

Too, Lillian

Feng Shui
Kuala Lumpur: Konsep Books, 1994

U

Unlawful Sex

Offences, Victims and Offenders in the Criminal Justice System of England and Wales
The Report of the Howard League Working Party
London: Waterloo Publishers Ltd., 1985

V

Van Gelder, Dora

The Real World of Fairies
A First-Person Account
Wheaton: Quest Books, 1999
First published in 1977

Vanguard, Thorkil

Phallós
A Symbol and its History in the Male World
New York: International Universities Press, 2001

Villoldo, Alberto

Healing States
A Journey Into the World of Spiritual Healing and Shamanism
With Stanley Krippner
New York: Simon & Schuster (Fireside), 1987

Dance of the Four Winds
Secrets of the Inca Medicine Wheel
With Eric Jendresen
Rochester: Destiny Books, 1995

Die Macht der vier Winde
Eine Reise ins Reich der Schamanen
München: Goldmann, 2009

Shaman, Healer, Sage
How to Heal Yourself and Others with the Energy Medicine
of the Americas
New York: Harmony, 2000

Hüter des alten Wissens
Schamanisches Heilen im Medizinrad
Darmstadt: Schirner Verlag, 2007

Healing the Luminous Body
The Way of the Shaman with Dr. Alberto Villoldo
DVD, Sacred Mysteries Productions, 2004

Mending The Past And Healing The Future with Soul Retrieval
New York: Hay House, 2005

Seelenrückholung: die Vergangenheit schamanistisch erkunden
Die Zukunft heilen
München, Goldmann, 2006

Vitebsky, Piers
The Shaman
Voyages of the Soul, Trance, Ecstasy and Healing from
Siberia to the Amazon
New York: Duncan Baird Publishers, 2001
Originally published in 1995

Von Riezler, Sigmund
Geschichte der Hexenprozesse in Bayern
Stuttgart: Magnus Verlag, 1983

W

Walker & Walker

The English Legal System
6th Edition, by R.J. Walker
London: Butterworths, 1985

Ward, Elizabeth

Father-Daughter Rape
New York: Grove Press, 1985

Watts, Alan W.

The Way of Zen
New York: Vintage Books, 1999

This Is It
And Other Essays on Zen and Spiritual Experience
New York: Vintage, 1973

Wee Chow Hou

The 36 Strategies of the Chinese
Adapting Ancient Chinese Wisdom to the Business World
New York: Addison-Wesley, 2007

Weiss, Jess E.

The Vestibule
New York: Ashley Books, 1979

West's Encyclopedia of American Law

Second Edition
New York: Gale Group, 2008

Wharton

Wharton's Criminal Law
14th ed. by Charles E. Torcia
Vol. II, §§99-282
Rochester, New York: The Lawyers Cooperative Publishing Co., 1979

What the Bleep Do We Know!?

See Arntz, William

Whiteman

Digest of International Law
Vol. 6
Washington, D.C.: Department of State Publication 8350, 1968

Whitfield, Charles L.

Healing the Child Within
Deerfield Beach, Fl: Health Communications, 1987

Whiting, Beatrice B.

Children of Six Cultures
A Psycho-Cultural Analysis
Cambridge: Harvard University Press, 1975

Wiener, Jon

Gimme Some Truth: The John Lennon FBI Files
Los Angeles: University of California Press, 1999

Wilber, Ken

Sex, Ecology, Spirituality
The Spirit of Evolution
Boston: Shambhala, 2000

Quantum Questions
Mystical Writings of The World's Greatest Physicists
Boston: Shambhala, 2001

Wild, Leon D.

The Runes Workbook
A Step-by-Step Guide to Learning the Wisdom of the Staves
San Diego: Thunder Bay Press, 2004

Wilhelm Helmut

The Wilhelm Lectures on the Book of Changes
Princeton: Princeton University Press, 1995

Wilhelm, Richard

The I Ching or Book of Changes
With C. Baynes
3rd Edition, Bollingen Series XIX
Princeton, NJ: Princeton University Press, 1967

Williams, Strephon Kaplan

Dreams and Spiritual Growth
With Patricia H. Berne and Louis M. Savary
New York: Paulist Press, 1984

Durch Traumarbeit zum eigenen Selbst
Die Jung-Senoi Methode
Interlaken: Ansata Verlag, 1987

Dream Cards
Understand Your Dreams and Enrich Your Life
New York: Simon & Schuster (Fireside), 1991

Wing, R. L.

The I Ching Workbook
Garden City, N.Y.: Doubleday, 1984

Das Arbeitsbuch zum I Ching
Mit Chinesischen Orakel Münzen
München: Goldmann, 2004

Het I Tjing Werkboek
Baarn: Bigot & Van Rossum, 1986

Woerly, Franz

Esprit Guide
Entretiens avec Karlfried Dürckheim
Paris: Albin Michel, 1985

Wolf, Fred Alan

Taking the Quantum Leap
The New Physics for Nonscientists
New York: Harper & Row, 1989

Der Quantensprung ist keine Hexerei
Frankfurt/M: Fischer Verlag, 1990

Parallel Universes
New York: Simon & Schuster, 1990

The Dreaming Universe
A Mind-Expanding Journey into the Realm Where
Psyche and Physics Meet
New York: Touchstone, 1995

The Eagle's Quest
A Physicist Finds the Scientific Truth At the Heart of the
Shamanic World
New York: Touchstone, 1997

Die Physik der Träume
Frankfurt/M: DTV Verlag, 1997

Mind into Matter
A New Alchemy of Science and Spirit
New York: Moment Point Press, 2000

Words and Phrases Legally Defined

Ed. By John Saunders
2nd Edition
London: Butterworths, 1969

Wydra, Nancilee

Feng Shui
The Book of Cures
Lincolnwood: Contemporary Books, 1996

Y

Yang, Jwing-Ming

Qigong, The Secret of Youth
Da Mo's Muscle/Tendon Changing and Marrow/Brain Washing Classics
Boston, Mass.: YMAA Publication Center, 2000

The Root of Chinese Qigong
Secrets for Health, Longevity, & Enlightenment
Roslindale, MA: YMAA Publication Center, 1997

Yates, Alayne

Sex Without Shame
Encouraging the Childs Healthy Sexual Development
New York, 1978
Republished Internet Edition

Yeats, William Butler

Irish Fairy and Folk Tales
New York: Modern Library, 2003

Mythologies
New York: Simon & Schuster, 1998
Author Copyright 1959, Renewed 1987 by Anne Yeats

Ywahoo, Dhyani

Voices of Our Ancestors
Cherokee Teachings from the Wisdom Fire
New York: Shambhala, 1987

Am Feuer der Weisheit
Lehren der Cherokee Indianer
Zürich: Theseus Verlag, 1988

Z

Znamenski, Andrei A.

Shamanism
Critical Concepts in Sociology
New York: Routledge, 2004

Zinker, Joseph

Se créer par la Gestalt
Montréal: Les Éditions de l'Homme, 1981

Zukav, Gary

The Dancing Wu Li Masters
An Overview of the New Physics
New York: HarperOne, 2001

Die tanzenden Wu Li Meister
Der östliche Pfad zum Verständnis der modernen Physik
Vom Quantensprung zum schwarzen Loch
Berlin: Rowohlt, 2000

Zweig, Stefan

Die Heilung durch den Geist
Mesmer, Mary Baker-Eddy, Freud
Frankfurt/M: Fischer Verlag, 1982
Originally published in 1931

Zyman, Sergio

The End of Marketing as We Know It
New York: HarperCollins, 2000

Das Ende der Marketing Mythen
Erfolgsrezepte des Aya-Cola für Umsatz und Profit
Berlin: Econ Verlag, 2000

To live happily is an inward power of the soul.
– Marcus Aurelius

FROM THE SAME AUTHOR

A Bibliography

You can search publications from here:
http://ipublica.com/books/

For audio books and music, you can start here:
http://ipublica.com/audio/

All paperbacks, audio downloads, audio book compact discs, music downloads and music compact discs, as well as Kindle books, are referenced on the site.

For free podcasts search in the 'Podcasts' section of iTunes under my author name.

For quoting my publications, please use the following form:
Pierre F. Walter, [Title]: [Subtitle], Newark: Sirius-C Media Galaxy LLC, 2012

English Publications

by Pierre F. Walter

Art & Photography Books

Culinary Pleasures in the Provence
Food Photography
Newark: Sirius-C Media Galaxy LLC, 2010
ISBN 978-1-461035-98-5

Jei's Art
Art Selected and Published by Pierre F. Walter
Newark: Sirius-C Media Galaxy LLC, 2010
ISBN 978-1-461036-82-1

The Spontaneous Art
A Short Guide to Immediate Creation
Newark: Sirius-C Media Galaxy LLC, 2010
ISBN 978-1-456594-89-3

Audio Books

A Psychological Revolution?
On the Teaching of J. Krishnamurti
Newark: Sirius-C Media Galaxy LLC, 2010
ISBN 978-1-933137-17-9

Child Play
Coaching Your Inner Child
Newark: Sirius-C Media Galaxy LLC, 2010
ISBN 978-1-933137-22-3

Consciousness and Shamanism

Theories of Causation and Cognitive Experiences
in the Ayahuasca Trance
Newark: Sirius-C Media Galaxy LLC, 2010
ISBN 978-1-933137-03-2

Creative Prayer

The Miracle Road
Newark: Sirius-C Media Galaxy LLC, 2010
ISBN 978-1-933137-23-0

Eight Dynamic Patterns of Living

Base Elements of True Civilization
Newark: Sirius-C Media Galaxy LLC, 2010
ISBN 978-1-933137-11-7

Emonics

A Systemic Analysis of Emotional Identity
in the Etiology of Sexual Paraphilias
Newark: Sirius-C Media Galaxy LLC, 2010
ISBN 978-1-933137-16-2

Emotional Flow

A Holistic Approach to Healing Sadism
Newark: Sirius-C Media Galaxy LLC, 2010
ISBN 978-1-933137-12-4

Love and Morality

A Study of the Roots of Violence
Newark: Sirius-C Media Galaxy LLC, 2010
ISBN 978-1-933137-13-1

Love or Laws?
When Law Punishes Life
Newark: Sirius-C Media Galaxy LLC, 2010
ISBN 978-1-933137-00-1

Minotaur Unveiled
A Historical Assessment of Adult-Child Sexual Interaction
Newark: Sirius-C Media Galaxy LLC, 2010
ISBN 978-1-933137-01-8

Notes on Consciousness
Elements of an Integrative Worldview
Newark: Sirius-C Media Galaxy LLC, 2010
ISBN 978-1-933137-04-9

Oedipal Hero
The Hidden Side of Glory
Newark: Sirius-C Media Galaxy LLC, 2010
ISBN 978-1-933137-15-5

Orgonomy and Schizophrenia
An Unpublished Case Report by Wilhelm Reich
Newark: Sirius-C Media Galaxy LLC, 2010
ISBN 978-1-933137-05-6

Patterns of Perception
Preferred Pathways to Genius
Newark: Sirius-C Media Galaxy LLC, 2010
ISBN 978-1-933137-06-3

Power or Depression?
The Cultural Roots of Abuse
Newark: Sirius-C Media Galaxy LLC, 2010
ISBN 978-1-933137-18-6

Processed Reality
Pitfalls of Perception and the Cosmic Mind
Newark: Sirius-C Media Galaxy LLC, 2010
ISBN 978-1-933137-14-8

Reich's Greatest Discoveries
An Essay on Wilhelm Reich
Newark: Sirius-C Media Galaxy LLC, 2010
ISBN 978-1-933137-07-0

Sane Child vs. Insane Society
Some Thoughts on Education
Newark: Sirius-C Media Galaxy LLC, 2010
ISBN 978-1-933137-19-3

Soul Jazz
Recognizing and Realizing Your Soul Values
Newark: Sirius-C Media Galaxy LLC, 2010
ISBN 978-1-933137-24-7

The Aquarius Age
What the Zodiac Reveals About the New Age
Newark: Sirius-C Media Galaxy LLC, 2010
ISBN 978-1-933137-67-4

The Drug Trap
Some Ideas Regarding Substance Abuse
Newark: Sirius-C Media Galaxy LLC, 2010
ISBN 978-1-933137-25-4

The Hero Culture
Annotations on Insanity
Newark: Sirius-C Media Galaxy LLC, 2010
ISBN 978-1-933137-38-4

The I Ching's Perennial Pro-Life Code
An Analysis of Pattern
Newark: Sirius-C Media Galaxy LLC, 2010
ISBN 978-1-933137-08-7

The Legal Split in Child Protection
Overcoming the Double Standard
Newark: Sirius-C Media Galaxy LLC, 2010
ISBN 978-1-933137-02-5

The Lunar Bull
Spiritual Significance of Matriarchy
Newark: Sirius-C Media Galaxy LLC, 2010
ISBN 978-1-933137-20-9

The Star Script
Astrology and Personal Growth
Newark: Sirius-C Media Galaxy LLC, 2010
ISBN 978-1-933137-26-1

The Webolution
A Publishing Highway?
Newark: Sirius-C Media Galaxy LLC, 2010
ISBN 978-1-933137-21-6

Awareness Guides

The Idiot Guide to Consciousness
Newark: Sirius-C Media Galaxy LLC, 2010
ISBN 978-1-453646-64-9

The Idiot Guide to Creativity and Career
Newark: Sirius-C Media Galaxy LLC, 2010
ISBN 978-1-453782-00-2

The Idiot Guide to Emotions
Newark: Sirius-C Media Galaxy LLC, 2010
ISBN 978-1-933137-48-3

The Idiot Guide to Intuition
Newark: Sirius-C Media Galaxy LLC, 2010
ISBN 978-1-453833-63-6

The Idiot Guide to Love
Newark: Sirius-C Media Galaxy LLC, 2010
ISBN 978-1-453833-63-6

The Idiot Guide to Sanity
Newark: Sirius-C Media Galaxy LLC, 2010
ISBN 978-1-453851-16-6

The Idiot Guide to Science
Newark: Sirius-C Media Galaxy LLC, 2010
ISBN 978-1-453862-29-2

The Idiot Guide to Servant Leadership
Newark: Sirius-C Media Galaxy LLC, 2010
ISBN 978-1-453765-89-0

The Idiot Guide to Soul Power
Newark: Sirius-C Media Galaxy LLC, 2010
ISBN 978-1-456349-78-3

The Idiot Guide to World Peace
Newark: Sirius-C Media Galaxy LLC, 2010
ISBN 978-1-456362-89-8

Book and DVD Reviews

110 Bestselling Books Reviewed by Pierre F. Walter
Newark: Sirius-C Media Galaxy LLC, 2010
ISBN 978-1-456505-00-4

The New Paradigm in Business, Marketing and Career
10 Bestselling Books Reviewed by Pierre F. Walter
Newark: Sirius-C Media Galaxy LLC, 2011
ISBN 978-1-468145-12-0

The New Paradigm in Consciousness and Psychology
53 Bestselling Books Reviewed by Pierre F. Walter
Newark: Sirius-C Media Galaxy LLC, 2011
ISBN 978-1-468156-50-8

The New Paradigm in Science and Systems Theory
40 Bestselling Books and DVDs Reviewed by Pierre F. Walter
Newark: Sirius-C Media Galaxy LLC, 2011
ISBN 978-1-468149-48-7

Encyclopedias

Academic Encyclopedia
Newark: Sirius-C Media Galaxy LLC, 2010
ISBN 978-1-453684-07-8

Illustrated Encyclopedia, Vol. 1 (Terms)
Newark: Sirius-C Media Galaxy LLC, 2010
ISBN 978-1-453687-32-1

Illustrated Encyclopedia, Vol. 2 (Personalities)
Newark: Sirius-C Media Galaxy LLC, 2010
ISBN 978-1-453784-05-1

Great Minds Series

Françoise Dolto and Language
Newark: Sirius-C Media Galaxy LLC, 2010
ISBN 978-1-453775-12-7

Fritjof Capra and the Systems View of Life
Newark: Sirius-C Media Galaxy LLC, 2010
ISBN 978-1-453684-07-8

Joseph Campbell and the Lunar Bull
Newark: Sirius-C Media Galaxy LLC, 2010
ISBN 978-1-453788-05-9

Monographs

Do You Love Einstein?
Creative Insights On Perennial Wisdom, Human Genius
and the Quantum Field
Newark: Sirius-C Media Galaxy LLC, 2010
ISBN 978-1-933137-55-1

Energy Science and Vibrational Healing
A Systems Approach Human Emotions and Sexuality
Newark: Sirius-C Media Galaxy LLC, 2010
ISBN 978-1-453729-91-5

Erós and Agapé
A Case of Healing the Split
Newark: Sirius-C Media Galaxy LLC, 2010
ISBN 978-1-456438-77-7

Evidence and Burden of Proof in Foreign Sovereign Immunity Litigation
A Guide for International Lawyers and Government Counsel
Newark: Sirius-C Media Galaxy LLC, 2010
ISBN 978-1-452890-41-8

Litigation Practice and Burden of Proof under the Foreign Sovereign Immunities Act, 1976
A Practical Guide for Business Lawyers and Government
Newark: Sirius-C Media Galaxy LLC, 2010
ISBN 978-1-453631-84-3

Love and Awareness
A Consciousness for the New Age
Newark: Sirius-C Media Galaxy LLC, 2010
ISBN 978-1-456365-04-2

Natural Order
Thesis, Antithesis and Synthesis in Human Evolution
Newark: Sirius-C Media Galaxy LLC, 2010
ISBN 978-1-453722-63-3

Normative Psychoanalysis
How the Oedipal Dogma Shapes Consumer Culture
Newark: Sirius-C Media Galaxy LLC, 2010
ISBN 978-1-453744-31-4

Sovereign Immunity Litigation in the United States and Canada
A Lawyer's Manual on Evidence and Burden of Proof for Every Phase of the Trial
Newark: Sirius-C Media Galaxy LLC, 2010
ISBN 978-1-453601-23-5

The Life Authoring Manual
An Integrated Approach to Personal Growth
Newark: Sirius-C Media Galaxy LLC, 2010
ISBN 978-1-453718-32-2

The Science of Orgonomy
A Study on Wilhelm Reich
Newark: Sirius-C Media Galaxy LLC, 2010
ISBN 978-1-456365-31-8

The Science of Shamanism
Millenary Model for an Integrative Worldview
Newark: Sirius-C Media Galaxy LLC, 2010
ISBN 978-1-45658-5853

Toward Social Change
A 12-Points Peace Agenda for Governments and Legal Counsel
Newark: Sirius-C Media Galaxy LLC, 2010
ISBN 978-1-456412-83-8

Poetic Writings and Audio Books

Poetic Writings
Stories, Pamphlets, Poetry, Changing the Love Pattern, The Hero Cult,
The Trial
Newark: Sirius-C Media Galaxy LLC, 2010
ISBN 978-1-453805-78-7

Mona Lisa Pamphlets (Audio Book)
Paraculture, Alkibiades, Princess Love
Newark: Sirius-C Media Galaxy LLC, 2010
ISBN 978-1-933137-40-7

Yami (Audio Book)
Short Story in Twelve Parts
Newark: Sirius-C Media Galaxy LLC, 2010
ISBN 978-1-933137-39-1

Scholarly Articles

Alternative Medicine and Wellness Techniques
14 Pathways to Health
Newark: Sirius-C Media Galaxy LLC, 2011
ISBN 978-1-466461-80-2

Aquarius Age and Publishing
A New Paradigm Emerging
Newark: Sirius-C Media Galaxy LLC, 2011
ISBN 978-1-468109-93-1

Basics of Career Design
Opening Inner Space
Newark: Sirius-C Media Galaxy LLC, 2011
ISBN 978-1-468118-67-4

Basics of Divination
How Divination Can Facilitate Smart Decision-Making
Newark: Sirius-C Media Galaxy LLC, 2011
ISBN 978-1-468122-12-1

Basics of Feng Shui
An Old Energy Science
Newark: Sirius-C Media Galaxy LLC, 2011
ISBN 978-1-468125-94-8

Basics of Mythology
Some Leading Archetypes
Newark: Sirius-C Media Galaxy LLC, 2011
ISBN 978-1-468129-13-7

Permissive Education
A Summary
Newark: Sirius-C Media Galaxy LLC, 2011
ISBN 978-1-468130-08-9

Taoism and the I Ching
Understanding Nonaction and Right Action
Newark: Sirius-C Media Galaxy LLC, 2011
ISBN 978-1-468131-22-2

The Inner Journey
Awakening Your Inner Artist
Newark: Sirius-C Media Galaxy LLC, 2011
ISBN 978-1-468131-03-1

The Mythology of Narcissism
Pathology of the Consumer Age
Newark: Sirius-C Media Galaxy LLC, 2011
ISBN 978-1-468133-52-3

The Secret Science
The Huna Knowledge of the Cosmic Energy Field
Newark: Sirius-C Media Galaxy LLC, 2011
ISBN 978-1-468137-25-5

French Publications

by Pierre F. Walter

Essais

Essais 1990-2010
Newark: Sirius-C Media Galaxy LLC, 2010
ISBN 978-1-453833-73-5

Écrits poétiques

Écrits poétiques
Newark: Sirius-C Media Galaxy LLC, 2010
ISBN 978-1-460984-51-2

Livres Audio

Anissia
Histoire vraie
Newark: Sirius-C Media Galaxy LLC, 2010
ISBN 978-1-933137-30-8

Le jardin infâme
Un regard sur l'âme et son corps
Newark: Sirius-C Media Galaxy LLC, 2010
ISBN 978-1-933137-33-9

Potentiel et créativité
Au sujet du développement de soi
Newark: Sirius-C Media Galaxy LLC, 2010
ISBN 978-1-933137-34-6

Relations sans fusion
Au sujet du développement de l'autonomie
Newark: Sirius-C Media Galaxy LLC, 2010
ISBN 978-1-933137-37-7

Une éducation amoureuse
Un regard sur l'enfant au naturel
Newark: Sirius-C Media Galaxy LLC, 2010
ISBN 978-1-933137-35-3

German Publications

by Pierre F. Walter

Audiobücher

Die Ödipale Kultur
Wege aus der Verstrickung
Newark: Sirius-C Media Galaxy LLC, 2010
ISBN 978-0-9760433-1-7

Fusion und Individuation
Von der Fusion zum eigenen Selbst
Newark: Sirius-C Media Galaxy LLC, 2010
ISBN 978-1-933137-65-0

Kaleidoskop der Emotionen
Ein Leitfaden zur Selbstfühlung
Newark: Sirius-C Media Galaxy LLC, 2010
ISBN 978-1-933137-66-7

Macht oder Ohnmacht
Erziehung zum Missbrauch
Newark: Sirius-C Media Galaxy LLC, 2010
ISBN 978-0-9760433-3-1

Wilhelm Reich und Orgonomie
Eine Einführung in Reichs Orgonforschung
Newark: Sirius-C Media Galaxy LLC, 2010
ISBN 978-0-9760433-6-2

Monographien

Essays 1990-2010
Zwanzig Jahre schriftstellerisches Engagement in den Bereichen
Bewusstsein, Friedensforschung, Musikologie, Orgonomie,
Kinderschutz, Gewaltverhütung und Persönlichkeitsentwicklung
Newark: Sirius-C Media Galaxy LLC, 2010
ISBN 978-1-456506-827

Mehr als Kindersex
Historische, Ethische, Ästhetische, Psychologische und Rechtliche
Aspekte der Kindliebe
Newark: Sirius-C Media Galaxy LLC, 2010
ISBN 978-1-933137-54-4

Poetische Schriften

Aphorismen, Gedichte, Balladen, Märchen
Gereimtes und Ungereimtes
Newark: Sirius-C Media Galaxy LLC, 2010
ISBN 978-1-456511-93-7

Dramatische Schriften
David und Jonathan / David H. oder die Liebe zur Fotografie / Das
Verfahren / Kurzdrehbücher und Sketche
Newark: Sirius-C Media Galaxy LLC, 2010
ISBN 978-1-456511-97-5

Kindheit, Ehe, Studien
Autobiographie 1955-1985
Newark: Sirius-C Media Galaxy LLC, 2010
ISBN 978-1-456512-35-4

Liebe und Philosophie
Gedanken, Notebook, Traktate
Newark: Sirius-C Media Galaxy LLC, 2010
ISBN 978-1-460945-11-7

Pamphlete und Monelle
'Monelle' von Marcel Schwob in der Übersetzung von Pierre F. Walter
Newark: Sirius-C Media Galaxy LLC, 2010
ISBN 978-1-460945-14-8

Romane und Novelletten
Erfundenes und Gesungenes
Newark: Sirius-C Media Galaxy LLC, 2010
ISBN 978-1-461036-94-4

Traktate (Audio Buch)
Eine Sammlung von Gesängen
Newark: Sirius-C Media Galaxy LLC, 2010
ISBN 978-1-933137-42-1

Wahre Geschichten
Newark: Sirius-C Media Galaxy LLC, 2010
ISBN 978-1-461037-01-9

Textbücher Lebensberatung (Bewusstseinsführer)

Wege zur Selbstentfaltung
Newark: Sirius-C Media Galaxy LLC, 2010
ISBN 978-1-456509-19-4

Wege zum Weltfrieden
Newark: Sirius-C Media Galaxy LLC, 2010
ISBN 978-1-456509-37-8

Web Presence

Pierre F. Walter on the Web

Sites

http://authoryourlife.com

http://ipublica.com

http://ipublica.net

http://ipublica.org

http://ipublica.tv

Video Channels

http://ipublica.net/vchannels/

http://youtube.com/user/ipublica

http://youtube.com/user/authoryourlife

http://vimeo.com/pierrefwalter/channels

http://ipublica.blip.tv/

http://authoryourlife.blip.tv/

http://emosexuality.blip.tv/

http://pierrefwalter.blip.tv/